SIMPLY PHILOSOPHICAL QUOTES

915 INSPIRING, THOUGHT PROVOKING QUOTES
FROM 10 INFLUENTIAL PHILOSOPHERS TO OPEN
YOUR THIRD EYE

ABSTRACT THOUGHTS

AT PUBLISHING

CONTENTS

CONFUCIUS

*C*onfucius was born circa 551 BC in Zou, modern Shandong, China. His father, Kong He (or Shuliang He), was an elderly commandant of the local Lu garrison. It has to be said that not a lot was actually known about the life that Confucius lived, but what we do know is that he was a Chinese philosopher as well as a politician of the Spring and Autumn period in China. Confucius supposedly disagreed with the morals and the ethics of the ruler of the time, as he was a distracted leader who was always chasing women and money. Confucius first found employment with the Jisun clan and assumed modest jobs such as livestock and granaries keeper. Because the family had served for decades as counsellors to the rulers of Lu, he was able to eventually work his way up to the minister of crime in the Lu government. When a major dispute between the government and other high-class families wanting to seize power ensued in 498 BC, Confucius was forced to leave Lu.

Confucius would leave his region and wander around much of north-east and central China for years. Over time he gained a following and people liked what he stood for. He spread his knowledge, wisdom, and teachings to his followers. Although he has no actual self-written literature, his teachings were documented by his followers, and the bodies of work would be known as *Analects*.

After Confucius died, his followers and students created schools across all of Asia and would then go on to spread his word for the following years.

Treating Parents with Reverence

Confucius believed that we should treat our parents with the utmost respect, obey them when we are young, and care for them when they grow old. Confucius also believed that we should always remain in closer proximity to our parents to ensure we can give a helping hand in case of an emergency. This outlook is known as filial piety, meaning to be good to one's parents, take care of one's parents; to engage in good conduct not just towards parents but also outside the home to bring a good name to one's parents and ancestors, display sorrow for their sickness and death and to bury them and carry out sacrifices after their death.

Confucius believed that this was a very important thing to do as he believed that our mortality and moral compass comes from our homes. He believed that for individuals to express good traits in society they must first master those traits at home, then those traits can be transferred with ease to society.

Obey Honourable People

Confucius, just like Aristotle, believed that the public figure we have in our society plays a massive role in the way we function together. Confucius believed that we should look up to people whose accomplishments massively outweigh our own. In doing so we can start to become more like these people. It's too often we glorify the wrong values, so having very accomplished individuals who are respected is an important part of a functioning society.

The Cultivation of Knowledge is More Important Than Creativity

Confucius was adamant that universal wisdom and the gathering of knowledge and understanding about how things work was one of the most important things in this life. He believed that we should all strive to reach these 5 constant virtues:

Benevolence, ritual propriety, righteousness, wisdom and integrity. Although men are born good, we must work hard at these virtues to mature ourselves and our nature.

5 Facts About Confucius

1. Confucius started his teaching career at the age of 24.
2. Confucius got married when he was 19.
3. The 25th day of the eighth lunar month in the Chinese calendar is Confucius's birthday, and this is celebrated in varying ways across East Asia.
4. Out of the 5000 students who were taught by him, only 72 students would go on to become 'wisemen'.
5. Confucianism is an ancient Chinese belief system that was founded by Confucius and is still around today.

99 CONFUCIUS QUOTES

"LEARN AVIDLY. QUESTION IT REPEATEDLY. ANALYSE IT CAREFULLY. THEN PUT WHAT YOU HAVE LEARNED INTO PRACTICE INTELLIGENTLY."

"THE MAN WHO SAYS HE CAN, AND THE MAN WHO SAYS HE CANNOT...ARE BOTH CORRECT."

"THE NOBLER SORT OF MAN EMPHASISES THE GOOD QUALITIES IN OTHERS, AND DOES NOT ACCENTUATE THE BAD. THE INFERIOR DOES."

"REAL KNOWLEDGE IS TO KNOW THE EXTENT OF ONE'S IGNORANCE."

"YOUR LIFE IS WHAT YOUR THOUGHTS MAKE IT."

"CHOOSE A JOB YOU LOVE, AND YOU WILL NEVER HAVE TO WORK A DAY IN YOUR LIFE."

"YOU ARE WHAT YOU THINK."

"LOOKING AT SMALL ADVANTAGES PREVENTS GREAT AFFAIRS FROM BEING ACCOMPLISHED."

"ALL PEOPLE ARE THE SAME; ONLY THEIR HABITS DIFFER."

"WE HAVE TWO LIVES, AND THE SECOND BEGINS WHEN WE REALISE WE ONLY HAVE ONE."

"THE MAN WHO ASKS A QUESTION IS A FOOL FOR A MINUTE, THE MAN WHO DOES NOT ASK IS A FOOL FOR LIFE."

"THE JOURNEY WITH A 1000 MILES BEGINS WITH A SINGLE STEP."

"WORRY NOT THAT NO ONE KNOWS YOU; SEEK TO BE WORTH KNOWING."

"THE MAN WHO MOVES A MOUNTAIN BEGINS BY CARRYING AWAY SMALL STONES."

"WHEN IT IS OBVIOUS THAT THE GOALS CANNOT BE REACHED, DON'T ADJUST THE GOALS, ADJUST THE ACTION STEPS."

"THE ESSENCE OF KNOWLEDGE IS, HAVING IT, TO USE IT."

"ONE JOY DISPELS A HUNDRED CARES."

"WHEN YOU SEE A GOOD PERSON, THINK OF BECOMING LIKE HER/HIM. WHEN YOU SEE SOMEONE NOT SO GOOD, REFLECT ON YOUR OWN WEAK POINTS."

"I SLEPT AND DREAMT LIFE IS BEAUTY, I WOKE AND FOUND LIFE IS DUTY."

"THEY MUST OFTEN CHANGE WHO WOULD REMAIN CONSTANT IN HAPPINESS AND WISDOM."

"DON'T COMPLAIN ABOUT THE SNOW ON YOUR NEIGHBOUR'S ROOF WHEN YOUR OWN DOORSTEP IS UNCLEAN."

"BEFORE YOU EMBARK ON A JOURNEY OF REVENGE, DIG TWO GRAVES."

"A LION CHASED ME UP A TREE, AND I GREATLY ENJOYED THE VIEW FROM THE TOP."

"IF YOU ARE THE SMARTEST PERSON IN THE ROOM, THEN YOU ARE IN THE WRONG ROOM."

"ACT WITH KINDNESS, BUT DO NOT EXPECT GRATITUDE."

"BE NOT ASHAMED OF MISTAKES AND THUS MAKE THEM CRIMES."

"THE SUPERIOR MAN IS MODEST IN HIS SPEECH, BUT EXCEEDS IN HIS ACTIONS."

"BE STRICT WITH YOURSELF BUT LEAST REPROACHFUL OF OTHERS AND COMPLAINT IS KEPT AFAR."

"ROADS WERE MADE FOR JOURNEYS, NOT DESTINATIONS."

"NO MATTER HOW BUSY YOU MAY THINK YOU ARE, YOU MUST FIND TIME FOR READING, OR SURRENDER YOURSELF TO SELF-CHOSEN IGNORANCE."

"BY NATURE, MEN ARE NEARLY ALIKE; BY PRACTICE, THEY GET TO BE WIDE APART."

"LEARN AS IF YOU WERE NOT REACHING YOUR GOAL AND AS THOUGH YOU WERE SCARED OF MISSING IT."

"NEVER CONTRACT FRIENDSHIP WITH A MAN THAT IS NOT BETTER THAN THYSELF."

"HE WHO KNOWS ALL THE ANSWERS HAS NOT BEEN ASKED ALL THE QUESTIONS."

"THOSE WHO CANNOT FORGIVE OTHERS BREAK THE BRIDGE OVER WHICH THEY THEMSELVES MUST PASS."

"THOSE WHO KNOW THE TRUTH ARE NOT EQUAL TO THOSE WHO LOVE IT."

"THE SUPERIOR MAN THINKS ALWAYS OF VIRTUE; THE COMMON MAN THINKS OF COMFORT."

"THINK OF TOMORROW, THE PAST CAN'T BE MENDED."

"RESPECT YOURSELF AND OTHERS WILL RESPECT YOU."

"TO BE WRONGED IS NOTHING, UNLESS YOU CONTINUE TO REMEMBER IT."

"I HEAR AND I FORGET. I SEE AND I REMEMBER. I DO AND I UNDERSTAND."

"THE SUPERIOR MAN ACTS BEFORE HE SPEAKS, AND AFTERWARDS SPEAKS ACCORDING TO HIS ACTION."

"SUCCESS DEPENDS UPON PREVIOUS PREPARATION, AND WITHOUT SUCH PREPARATION THERE IS SURE TO BE FAILURE."

"ONLY THE WISEST AND STUPIDEST OF MEN NEVER CHANGE."

"STUDY THE PAST IF YOU WOULD DEFINE THE FUTURE."

"OUR GREATEST GLORY IS NOT IN NEVER FALLING, BUT IN RISING EVERY TIME WE FALL."

"LEARNING WITHOUT THOUGHT IS LABOUR LOST; THOUGHT WITHOUT LEARNING IS PERILOUS."

"DO NOT IMPOSE ON OTHERS WHAT YOU YOURSELF DO NOT DESIRE."

"THE SUPERIOR MAN MAKES THE DIFFICULTY TO BE OVERCOME HIS FIRST INTEREST; SUCCESS ONLY COMES LATER."

"IF YOU MAKE A MISTAKE AND DO NOT CORRECT IT, THIS IS CALLED A MISTAKE."

"EDUCATION BREEDS CONFIDENCE. CONFIDENCE BREEDS HOPE. HOPE BREEDS PEACE."

"A SUPERIOR MAN IS MODEST IN HIS SPEECH, BUT EXCEEDS IN HIS ACTIONS."

"TO SEE THE RIGHT AND NOT TO DO IT IS COWARDICE."

"VIRTUOUS PEOPLE OFTEN REVENGE THEMSELVES FOR THE CONSTRAINTS TO WHICH THEY SUBMIT BY THE BOREDOM WHICH THEY INSPIRE."

"HE WHO ACTS WITH A CONSTANT VIEW TO HIS OWN ADVANTAGE WILL BE MUCH MURMURED AGAINST."

"THE SUPERIOR MAN IS DISTRESSED BY THE LIMITATIONS OF HIS ABILITY; HE IS NOT DISTRESSED BY THE FACT THAT MEN DO NOT RECOGNISE THE ABILITY THAT HE HAS."

"TO SEE WHAT IS RIGHT AND NOT TO DO IT IS WANT OF COURAGE, OR OF PRINCIPLE."

"WHEN ANGER RISES, THINK OF THE CONSEQUENCES."

"IN A COUNTRY WELL-GOVERNED, POVERTY IS SOMETHING TO BE ASHAMED OF. IN A COUNTRY BADLY GOVERNED, WEALTH IS SOMETHING TO BE ASHAMED OF."

"TO KNOW WHAT YOU KNOW AND WHAT YOU DO NOT KNOW, THAT IS TRUE KNOWLEDGE."

"I WANT YOU TO BE EVERYTHING THAT'S YOU, DEEP AT THE CENTRE OF YOUR BEING."

"THE OBJECT OF THE SUPERIOR MAN IS TRUTH."

"WHEN YOU HAVE FAULTS, DO NOT FEAR TO ABANDON THEM."

"TO GO BEYOND IS AS WRONG AS TO FALL SHORT."

"IF YOU THINK IN TERMS OF A YEAR, PLANT A SEED; IF IN TERMS OF TEN YEARS, PLANT TREES; IF IN TERMS OF 100 YEARS, TEACH THE PEOPLE."

"IF YOU LOOK INTO YOUR OWN HEART, AND YOU FIND NOTHING WRONG THERE, WHAT IS THERE TO WORRY ABOUT? WHAT IS THERE TO FEAR?"

"IT DOES NOT MATTER HOW SLOWLY YOU GO AS LONG AS YOU DO NOT STOP."

"VIRTUE IS NOT LEFT TO STAND ALONE. HE WHO PRACTICES IT WILL HAVE NEIGHBOURS."

"BETTER A DIAMOND WITH A FLAW THAN A PEBBLE WITHOUT."

"THE SUPERIOR MAN DOES NOT, EVEN FOR THE SPACE OF A SINGLE MEAL, ACT CONTRARY TO VIRTUE. IN MOMENTS OF HASTE, HE CLEAVES TO IT. IN SEASONS OF DANGER, HE CLEAVES TO IT."

"THE WILL TO WIN, THE DESIRE TO SUCCEED, THE URGE TO REACH YOUR FULL POTENTIAL... THESE ARE THE KEYS THAT WILL UNLOCK THE DOOR TO PERSONAL EXCELLENCE."

"GO BEFORE THE PEOPLE WITH YOUR EXAMPLE, AND BE LABORIOUS IN THEIR AFFAIRS."

"WHEN WE SEE PERSONS OF WORTH, WE SHOULD THINK OF EQUALLING THEM; WHEN WE SEE PERSONS OF A CONTRARY CHARACTER, WE SHOULD TURN INWARDS AND EXAMINE OURSELVES."

"IF WE DON'T KNOW LIFE, HOW CAN WE KNOW DEATH?"

"THE EXPECTATIONS OF LIFE DEPEND UPON DILIGENCE; THE MECHANIC THAT WOULD PERFECT HIS WORK MUST FIRST SHARPEN HIS TOOLS."

"HE WHO SPEAKS WITHOUT MODESTY WILL FIND IT DIFFICULT TO MAKE HIS WORDS GOOD."

"WHAT YOU DO NOT WANT DONE TO YOURSELF, DO NOT DO TO OTHERS."

"WITHOUT FEELINGS OF RESPECT, WHAT IS THERE TO DISTINGUISH MEN FROM BEASTS?"

"YOU CANNOT OPEN A BOOK WITHOUT LEARNING SOMETHING."

"A GENTLEMAN WOULD BE ASHAMED SHOULD HIS DEEDS NOT MATCH HIS WORDS."

"WHEN A PERSON SHOULD BE SPOKEN WITH, AND YOU DON'T SPEAK WITH THEM, YOU LOSE THEM. WHEN A PERSON SHOULDN'T BE SPOKEN WITH AND YOU SPEAK TO THEM, YOU WASTE YOUR BREATH. THE WISE DO NOT LOSE PEOPLE, NOR DO THEY WASTE THEIR BREATH."

"TO SEE AND LISTEN TO THE WICKED IS ALREADY THE BEGINNING OF WICKEDNESS."

"WHEREVER YOU GO, GO WITH ALL YOUR HEART."

"GIVE A BOWL OF RICE TO A MAN AND YOU WILL FEED HIM FOR A DAY. TEACH HIM HOW TO GROW HIS OWN RICE AND YOU WILL SAVE HIS LIFE."

"IT IS MORE SHAMEFUL TO DISTRUST OUR FRIENDS THAN TO BE DECEIVED BY THEM."

"LIFE IS REALLY SIMPLE, BUT WE INSIST ON MAKING IT COMPLICATED."

"SILENCE IS A TRUE FRIEND WHO NEVER BETRAYS."

"BY THREE METHODS WE MAY LEARN WISDOM: FIRST, BY REFLECTION, WHICH IS NOBLEST; SECOND, BY IMITATION, WHICH IS EASIEST; AND THIRD BY EXPERIENCE, WHICH IS THE BITTEREST."

"WISDOM, COMPASSION, AND COURAGE ARE THE THREE UNIVERSALLY RECOGNISED MORAL QUALITIES OF MEN."

"DEATH AND LIFE HAVE THEIR DETERMINED APPOINTMENTS; RICHES AND HONOURS DEPEND UPON HEAVEN."

"EVERYTHING HAS BEAUTY, BUT NOT EVERYONE SEES IT."

"THE MORE MAN MEDITATES UPON GOOD THOUGHTS, THE BETTER WILL BE HIS WORLD AND THE WORLD AT LARGE."

"HE WHO LEARNS BUT DOES NOT THINK, IS LOST! HE WHO THINKS BUT DOES NOT LEARN IS IN GREAT DANGER."

"IT IS EASY TO HATE AND IT IS DIFFICULT TO LOVE. THIS IS HOW THE WHOLE SCHEME OF THINGS WORKS. ALL GOOD THINGS ARE DIFFICULT TO ACHIEVE; AND BAD THINGS ARE VERY EASY TO GET."

"THE STRENGTH OF A NATION DERIVES FROM THE INTEGRITY OF THE HOME."

"THE SUPERIOR MAN UNDERSTANDS WHAT IS RIGHT; THE INFERIOR MAN UNDERSTANDS WHAT WILL SELL."

"NEVER GIVE A SWORD TO A MAN WHO CAN'T DANCE."

"WE SHOULD FEEL SORROW, BUT NOT SINK UNDER ITS OPPRESSION."

"IMAGINATION IS MORE IMPORTANT THAN KNOWLEDGE."

"WHEN YOU KNOW A THING, TO HOLD THAT YOU KNOW IT; AND WHEN YOU DO NOT KNOW A THING, TO ALLOW THAT YOU DO NOT KNOW IT – THIS IS KNOWLEDGE."

IMMANUEL KANT

*I*mmanuel Kant was a German philosopher and a central enlightenment thinker; he was born in April 1724. He amassed a very impressive and respectable portfolio with many systematic works on epistemology, metaphysics, ethics and aesthetics. Kant grew up modestly with his father being a shoemaker. He found employment as a family tutor and was employed by three different families over nine years. It was only in his 50s that Kant became a very successful and popular professor. Kant was brought up in a very strict and religious household but dropped his child-hood religious beliefs as he got older. He did, however, appreciate the fact that religion did a great job in providing a coping mechanism for his parents during times of struggle, and thus he viewed religion this way, as a coping mechanism for people. Kant would go on to live into his old age, dying in 1804.

The Categorical Imperative

The categorical imperative was first mentioned in his writing in the groundwork of the metaphysics of morals. In a sense, the categorical imperative is a premise which Kant believed should be at the centre of one's logic when faced with a difficult choice.

The categorical imperative states that one must 'act only according to that maxim by which you can at the same time will if that should become a universal law'. What Kant meant by this is that when we are faced with a difficult choice like sleeping with our neighbour's wife, we must first ask ourselves if we would want to live in a world where this was always happening and was the acceptable thing to do.

Value in Existence

We should always treat people always as ends and never as a means. If a person is an end, it means their inherent value doesn't depend on anything else - it doesn't depend on whether the person is enjoying their life or making other people's lives better. We exist, so we have value. The idea is often brought up in discussions of animal rights, with the idea that if they have rights, animals must be treated as ends in themselves.

The Meaning of Freedom

Kant believed that the central duty of a government should be to bring liberty to the nation by encouraging people to take action that takes them closer to their free selves. We are free when our actions align with our best feelings of love, compassion and kindness. On the other hand, we only become slaves when we give in to our primitive, animalistic feelings of aggression, hate and envy. Kant taught that we must always work on ourselves to become more rational and sovereign.

5 Facts About Immanuel Kant

1. Kant received a doctorate in philosophy in 1755.
2. Kant was born in the province of Koenigsberg, and would never move out through his whole life.
3. His parents were devout Lutherans.

4. One of Kant's very close friends helped finance his education.

5. *The Republic,* arguably Kant's most famous work, was published when he was 57 years old.

72 IMMANUEL KANT QUOTES

"LOOK CLOSELY. THE BEAUTIFUL MAY BE SMALL."

"HE WHO IS CRUEL TO ANIMALS BECOMES HARD ALSO IN HIS DEALINGS WITH MEN. WE CAN JUDGE THE HEART OF A MAN BY HIS TREATMENT OF ANIMALS."

"I HAD TO DENY KNOWLEDGE IN ORDER TO MAKE ROOM FOR FAITH."

"ALL OUR KNOWLEDGE BEGINS WITH THE SENSES, PROCEEDS THEN TO THE UNDERSTANDING, AND ENDS WITH REASON. THERE IS NOTHING HIGHER THAN REASON."

"WHEREAS THE BEAUTIFUL IS LIMITED, THE SUBLIME IS LIMITLESS, SO THAT THE MIND IN THE PRESENCE OF THE SUBLIME, ATTEMPTING TO IMAGINE WHAT IT CANNOT, HAS PAIN IN THE FAILURE BUT PLEASURE IN CONTEMPLATING THE IMMENSITY OF THE ATTEMPT."

"FOR PEACE TO REIGN ON EARTH, HUMANS MUST EVOLVE INTO NEW BEINGS WHO HAVE LEARNED TO SEE THE WHOLE FIRST."

"RULES FOR HAPPINESS: SOMETHING TO DO, SOMEONE TO LOVE, SOMETHING TO HOPE FOR."

"THE BUSIER WE ARE, THE MORE ACUTELY WE FEEL THAT WE LIVE, THE MORE CONSCIOUS WE ARE OF LIFE."

"GENIUS IS THE ABILITY TO INDEPENDENTLY ARRIVE AT AND UNDERSTAND CONCEPTS THAT WOULD NORMALLY HAVE TO BE TAUGHT BY ANOTHER PERSON."

"THAT THE STEP TO COMPETENCE IS HELD TO BE VERY DANGEROUS BY THE FAR GREATER PORTION OF MANKIND..."

"THE DEATH OF DOGMA IS THE BIRTH OF MORALITY."

"SPACE AND TIME ARE THE FRAMEWORK WITHIN WHICH THE MIND IS CONSTRAINED TO CONSTRUCT ITS EXPERIENCE OF REALITY."

"THOUGHTS WITHOUT CONTENT ARE EMPTY, INTUITIONS WITHOUT CONCEPTS ARE BLIND."

"BUT TO UNITE IN A PERMANENT RELIGIOUS INSTITUTION WHICH IS NOT TO BE SUBJECT TO DOUBT BEFORE THE PUBLIC EVEN IN THE LIFETIME OF ONE MAN, AND THEREBY TO MAKE A PERIOD OF TIME FRUITLESS IN THE PROGRESS OF MANKIND TOWARD IMPROVEMENT, THUS WORKING TO THE DISADVANTAGE OF POSTERITY - THAT IS ABSOLUTELY FORBIDDEN. FOR HIMSELF (AND ONLY FOR A SHORT TIME) A MAN MAY POSTPONE ENLIGHTENMENT IN WHAT HE OUGHT TO KNOW, BUT TO RENOUNCE IT FOR POSTERITY IS TO INJURE AND TRAMPLE ON THE RIGHTS OF MANKIND."

"THE READING OF ALL GOOD BOOKS IS LIKE A CONVERSATION WITH THE FINEST MINDS OF PAST CENTURIES."

"ACT ONLY ACCORDING TO THAT MAXIM WHEREBY YOU CAN AT THE SAME TIME WILL THAT IT SHOULD BECOME A UNIVERSAL LAW."

"AN AGE CANNOT BIND ITSELF AND ORDAIN TO PUT THE SUCCEEDING ONE INTO SUCH A CONDITION THAT IT CANNOT EXTEND ITS (AT BEST VERY OCCASIONAL) KNOWLEDGE , PURIFY ITSELF OF ERRORS, AND PROGRESS IN GENERAL ENLIGHTENMENT. THAT WOULD BE A CRIME AGAINST HUMAN NATURE, THE PROPER DESTINATION OF WHICH LIES PRECISELY IN THIS PROGRESS AND THE DESCENDANTS WOULD BE FULLY JUSTIFIED IN REJECTING THOSE DECREES AS HAVING BEEN MADE IN AN UNWARRANTED AND MALICIOUS MANNER."

"THE TOUCHSTONE OF EVERYTHING THAT CAN BE CONCLUDED AS A LAW FOR A PEOPLE LIES IN THE QUESTION WHETHER THE PEOPLE COULD HAVE IMPOSED SUCH A LAW ON ITSELF."

"THE LIGHT DOVE, IN FREE FLIGHT CUTTING THROUGH THE AIR THE RESISTANCE OF WHICH IT FEELS, COULD GET THE IDEA THAT IT COULD DO EVEN BETTER IN AIRLESS SPACE. LIKEWISE, PLATO ABANDONED THE WORLD OF THE SENSES BECAUSE IT POSED SO MANY HINDRANCES FOR THE UNDERSTANDING, AND DARED TO GO BEYOND IT ON THE WINGS OF THE IDEAS, IN THE EMPTY SPACE OF PURE UNDERSTANDING."

"MAN MUST BE DISCIPLINED, FOR HE IS BY NATURE RAW AND WILD.."

"SKEPTICISM IS THUS A RESTING-PLACE FOR HUMAN REASON, WHERE IT CAN REFLECT UPON ITS DOGMATIC WANDERINGS AND MAKE SURVEY OF THE REGION IN WHICH IT FINDS ITSELF, SO THAT FOR THE FUTURE IT MAY BE ABLE TO CHOOSE ITS PATH WITH MORE CERTAINTY. BUT IT IS NO DWELLING-PLACE FOR PERMANENT SETTLEMENT. SUCH CAN BE OBTAINED ONLY THROUGH PERFECT CERTAINTY IN OUR KNOWLEDGE, ALIKE OF THE OBJECTS THEMSELVES AND OF THE LIMITS WITHIN WHICH ALL OUR KNOWLEDGE OF OBJECTS IS ENCLOSED."

"AS NATURE HAS UNCOVERED FROM UNDER THIS HARD SHELL THE SEED FOR WHICH SHE MOST TENDERLY CARES - THE PROPENSITY AND VOCATION TO FREE THINKING - THIS GRADUALLY WORKS BACK UPON THE CHARACTER OF THE PEOPLE, WHO THEREBY GRADUALLY BECOME CAPABLE OF MANAGING FREEDOM; FINALLY, IT AFFECTS THE PRINCIPLES OF GOVERNMENT, WHICH FINDS IT TO ITS ADVANTAGE TO TREAT MEN, WHO ARE NOW MORE THAN MACHINES, IN ACCORDANCE WITH THEIR DIGNITY."

"IN ALL JUDGEMENTS BY WHICH WE DESCRIBE ANYTHING AS BEAUTIFUL, WE ALLOW NO ONE TO BE OF ANOTHER OPINION."

"ENLIGHTENMENT IS MAN'S EMERGENCE FROM HIS SELF-INCURRED IMMATURITY."

"MARRIAGE...IS THE UNION OF TWO PEOPLE OF DIFFERENT SEXES WITH A VIEW TO THE MUTUAL POSSESSION OF EACH OTHER'S SEXUAL ATTRIBUTES FOR THE DURATION OF THEIR LIVES."

"BUT ALTHOUGH ALL OUR KNOWLEDGE BEGINS WITH EXPERIENCE, IT DOES NOT FOLLOW THAT IT ARISES FROM EXPERIENCE."

"MORALITY IS NOT PROPERLY THE DOCTRINE OF HOW WE MAY MAKE OURSELVES HAPPY, BUT HOW WE MAY MAKE OURSELVES WORTHY OF HAPPINESS."

"AN ACTION, TO HAVE MORAL WORTH, MUST BE DONE FROM DUTY."

"IF THE TRUTH SHALL KILL THEM, LET THEM DIE."

"ONLY THE DESCENT INTO THE HELL OF SELF-KNOWLEDGE CAN PAVE THE WAY TO GODLINESS."

"WITHOUT MAN AND HIS POTENTIAL FOR MORAL PROGRESS, THE WHOLE OF REALITY WOULD BE A MERE WILDERNESS, A THING IN VAIN, AND HAVE NO FINAL PURPOSE."

"THE PEOPLE NATURALLY ADHERE MOST TO DOCTRINES WHICH DEMAND THE LEAST SELF-EXERTION AND THE LEAST USE OF THEIR OWN REASON, AND WHICH CAN BEST ACCOMMODATE THEIR DUTIES TO THEIR INCLINATIONS."

"A GOOD WILL IS GOOD NOT BECAUSE OF
WHAT IT EFFECTS, OR ACCOMPLISHES, NOT
BECAUSE OF ITS FITNESS TO ATTAIN SOME
INTENDED END, BUT GOOD JUST BY ITS
WILLING, I.E. IN ITSELF; AND, CONSIDERED
BY ITSELF, IT IS TO BE ESTEEMED BEYOND
COMPARE MUCH HIGHER THAN ANYTHING
THAT COULD EVER BE BROUGHT ABOUT BY
IT IN FAVOUR OF SOME INCLINATIONS, AND
INDEED, IF YOU WILL, THE SUM OF ALL
INCLINATIONS. EVEN IF BY SOME
PARTICULAR DISFAVOUR OF FATE, OR BY
THE SCANTY ENDOWMENT OF A STEP-
MOTHERLY NATURE, THIS WILL SHOULD
ENTIRELY LACK THE CAPACITY TO CARRY
THROUGH ITS PURPOSE; IF DESPITE ITS
GREATEST STRIVING IT SHOULD STILL
ACCOMPLISH NOTHING, AND ONLY THE
GOOD WILL WERE TO REMAIN (NOT OF
COURSE, AS A MERE WISH, BUT AS THE
SUMMONING OF ALL MEANS THAT ARE
WITHIN OUR CONTROL); THEN, LIKE A
JEWEL, IT WOULD STILL SHINE BY ITSELF,
AS SOMETHING THAT HAS FULL WORTH IN
ITSELF."

"IT WAS THE DUTY OF PHILOSOPHY TO DESTROY THE ILLUSIONS WHICH HAD THEIR ORIGIN IN MISCONCEPTIONS, WHATEVER DARLING HOPES AND VALUED EXPECTATIONS MAY BE RUINED BY ITS EXPLANATIONS."

"ALL FALSE ART, ALL VAIN WISDOM, LASTS ITS TIME BUT FINALLY DESTROYS ITSELF, AND ITS HIGHEST CULTURE IS ALSO THE EPOCH OF ITS DECAY."

"STANDING ARMIES CONSTANTLY THREATEN OTHER NATIONS WITH WAR BY GIVING THE APPEARANCE THAT THEY ARE PREPARED FOR IT, WHICH GOADS NATIONS INTO COMPETING WITH ONE ANOTHER IN THE NUMBER OF MEN UNDER ARMS, AND THIS PRACTICE KNOWS NO BOUNDS. AND SINCE THE COSTS RELATED TO MAINTAINING PEACE WILL IN THIS WAY FINALLY BECOME GREATER THAN THOSE OF A SHORT WAR, STANDING ARMIES ARE THE CAUSE OF WARS OF AGGRESSION THAT ARE INTENDED TO END BURDENSOME EXPENDITURES. MOREOVER, PAYING MEN TO KILL OR BE KILLED APPEARS TO USE THEM AS MERE MACHINES AND TOOLS IN THE HANDS OF ANOTHER (THE NATION), WHICH IS INCONSISTENT WITH THE RIGHTS OF HUMANITY."

"NATURE IS BEAUTIFUL BECAUSE IT LOOKS LIKE ART; AND ART CAN ONLY BE CALLED BEAUTIFUL IF WE ARE CONSCIOUS OF IT AS ART WHILE YET IT LOOKS LIKE NATURE."

"IN THE KINGDOM OF ENDS EVERYTHING HAS EITHER A PRICE OR A DIGNITY. WHAT HAS A PRICE CAN BE REPLACED BY SOMETHING ELSE AS ITS EQUIVALENT; WHAT ON THE OTHER HAND IS RAISED ABOVE ALL PRICE AND THEREFORE ADMITS OF NO EQUIVALENT HAS A DIGNITY."

"THE SCHEMATICS BY WHICH OUR UNDERSTANDING DEALS WITH THE PHENOMENAL WORLD ... IS A SKILL SO DEEPLY HIDDEN IN THE HUMAN SOUL THAT WE SHALL HARDLY GUESS THE SECRET TRICK THAT NATURE HERE EMPLOYS."

"BEAUTY PRESENTS AN INDETERMINATE CONCEPT OF UNDERSTANDING, THE SUBLIME AN INDETERMINATE CONCEPT OF REASON."

"EXPERIENCE WITHOUT THEORY IS BLIND, BUT THEORY WITHOUT EXPERIENCE IS MERE INTELLECTUAL PLAY."

"DIGNITY IS A VALUE THAT CREATES IRREPLACEABILITY."

"IT IS THE LAND OF TRUTH (ENCHANTED NAME!), SURROUNDED BY A WIDE AND STORMY OCEAN, THE TRUE HOME OF ILLUSION, WHERE MANY A FOG BANK AND ICE, THAT SOON MELTS AWAY, TEMPT US TO BELIEVE IN NEW LANDS, WHILE CONSTANTLY DECEIVING THE ADVENTUROUS MARINER WITH VAIN HOPES, AND INVOLVING HIM IN ADVENTURES WHICH HE CAN NEVER LEAVE, YET NEVER BRING TO AN END."

"SIMPLY TO ACQUIESCE IN SKEPTICISM CAN NEVER SUFFICE TO OVERCOME THE RESTLESSNESS OF REASON."

"IN EVERY DEPARTMENT OF PHYSICAL SCIENCE THERE IS ONLY SO MUCH SCIENCE, PROPERLY SO-CALLED, AS THERE IS MATHEMATICS."

"BY A LIE A MAN THROWS AWAY, AND AS IT WERE, ANNIHILATES HIS DIGNITY AS A MAN."

"OUR AGE IS THE AGE OF CRITICISM, TO WHICH EVERYTHING MUST BE SUBJECTED. THE SACREDNESS OF RELIGION, AND THE AUTHORITY OF LEGISLATION, ARE BY MANY REGARDED AS GROUNDS OF EXEMPTION FROM THE EXAMINATION OF THIS TRIBUNAL. BUT, IF THEY ARE EXEMPTED, THEY BECOME THE SUBJECTS OF JUST SUSPICION, AND CANNOT LAY CLAIM TO SINCERE RESPECT, WHICH REASON ACCORDS ONLY TO THAT WHICH HAS STOOD THE TEST OF A FREE AND PUBLIC EXAMINATION."

"BETTER THE WHOLE PEOPLE PERISH THAN THAT INJUSTICE BE DONE."

"WHAT MIGHT BE SAID OF THINGS IN THEMSELVES, SEPARATED FROM ALL RELATIONSHIPS TO OUR SENSES, REMAINS FOR US ABSOLUTELY UNKNOWN."

"ENLIGHTENMENT IS MAN'S EMERGENCE FROM HIS SELF-IMPOSED NONAGE. NONAGE IS THE INABILITY TO USE ONE'S OWN UNDERSTANDING WITHOUT ANOTHER'S GUIDANCE. THIS NONAGE IS SELF-IMPOSED IF ITS CAUSE LIES NOT IN LACK OF UNDERSTANDING BUT IN INDECISION AND LACK OF COURAGE TO USE ONE'S OWN MIND WITHOUT ANOTHER'S GUIDANCE. DARE TO KNOW! (SAPERE AUDE) "HAVE THE COURAGE TO USE YOUR OWN UNDERSTANDING," IS THEREFORE THE MOTTO OF THE ENLIGHTENMENT."

"MATHEMATICS, NATURAL SCIENCE, LAWS, ARTS, EVEN MORALITY, DO NOT COMPLETELY FILL THE SOUL; THERE IS ALWAYS A SPACE LEFT OVER RESERVED FOR PURE AND SPECULATIVE REASON, THE EMPTINESS OF WHICH PROMPTS US TO SEEK IN VAGARIES, BUFFOONERIES, AND MYSTICISM FOR WHAT SEEMS TO BE EMPLOYMENT AND ENTERTAINMENT, BUT WHAT ACTUALLY IS MERE PASTIME UNDERTAKEN IN ORDER TO DEADEN THE TROUBLESOME VOICE OF REASON, WHICH, IN ACCORDANCE WITH ITS NATURE, REQUIRES SOMETHING THAT CAN SATISFY IT AND DOES NOT MERELY SUBSERVE OTHER ENDS OR THE INTERESTS OF OUR INCLINATIONS."

"AS A MATTER OF FACT, NO OTHER
LANGUAGE IN THE WORLD HAS RECEIVED
SUCH PRAISE AS THE LITHUANIAN
LANGUAGE. THE GARLANDS OF HIGH
HONOUR HAVE BEEN TAKEN TO LITHUANIAN
PEOPLE FOR INVENTING, ELABORATING,
AND INTRODUCING THE MOST HIGHLY
DEVELOPED HUMAN SPEECH WITH ITS
BEAUTIFUL AND CLEAR PHONOLOGY.
MOREOVER, ACCORDING TO COMPARATIVE
PHILOLOGY, THE LITHUANIAN LANGUAGE IS
BEST QUALIFIED TO REPRESENT THE
PRIMITIVE ARYAN CIVILISATION AND
CULTURE."

"A CATEGORICAL IMPERATIVE WOULD BE
ONE WHICH REPRESENTED AN ACTION AS
OBJECTIVELY NECESSARY IN ITSELF,
WITHOUT REFERENCE TO ANY OTHER
PURPOSE."

"HUMAN REASON, IN ONE SPHERE OF ITS COGNITION, IS CALLED UPON TO CONSIDER QUESTIONS, WHICH IT CANNOT DECLINE, AS THEY ARE PRESENTED BY ITS OWN NATURE, BUT WHICH IT CANNOT ANSWER, AS THEY TRANSCEND EVERY FACULTY OF THE MIND."

"BUT, ABOVE ALL, IT WILL CONFER AN INESTIMABLE BENEFIT ON MORALITY AND RELIGION, BY SHOWING THAT ALL THE OBJECTIONS URGED AGAINST THEM MAY BE SILENCED FOREVER BY THE *SOCRATIC* METHOD, THAT IS TO SAY, BY PROVING THE IGNORANCE OF THE OBJECTOR."

"ALL HUMAN COGNITION BEGINS WITH INTUITIONS, PROCEEDS FROM THENCE TO CONCEPTIONS, AND ENDS WITH IDEAS."

"THE WHOLE INTEREST OF MY REASON, WHETHER SPECULATIVE OR PRACTICAL, IS CONCENTRATED IN THE THREE FOLLOWING QUESTIONS: WHAT CAN I KNOW? WHAT SHOULD I DO? WHAT MAY I HOPE?"

"SETTLE, FOR SURE AND UNIVERSALLY,
WHAT CONDUCT WILL PROMOTE THE
HAPPINESS OF A RATIONAL BEING."

"WHEN THE TREMULOUS RADIANCE OF A
SUMMER NIGHT FILLS WITH TWINKLING
STARS AND THE MOON ITSELF IS FULL, I AM
SLOWLY DRAWN INTO A STATE OF
ENHANCED SENSITIVITY, MADE OF
FRIENDSHIP AND DISDAIN FOR THE WORLD
AND ETERNITY."

"HIGH TOWERS, AND METAPHYSICALLY-
GREAT MEN RESEMBLING THEM, ROUND
BOTH OF WHICH THERE IS COMMONLY
MUCH WIND, ARE NOT FOR ME. MY PLACE IS
THE FRUITFUL BATHOS, THE BOTTOM-LAND,
OF EXPERIENCE; AND THE WORD
TRANSCENDENTAL, DOES NOT SIGNIFY
SOMETHING PASSING BEYOND ALL
EXPERIENCE, BUT SOMETHING THAT
INDEED PRECEDES IT A PRIORI, BUT THAT IS
INTENDED SIMPLY TO MAKE COGNITION OF
EXPERIENCE POSSIBLE."

"MAN, AND IN GENERAL EVERY RATIONAL BEING, EXISTS AS AN END IN HIMSELF, NOT MERELY AS A MEANS FOR ARBITRARY USE BY THIS OR THAT WILL: HE MUST IN ALL HIS ACTIONS, WHETHER THEY ARE DIRECTED TO HIMSELF OR TO OTHER RATIONAL BEINGS, ALWAYS BE VIEWED AT THE SAME TIME AS AN END."

"ANARCHY IS LAW AND FREEDOM WITHOUT FORCE."

"DESPOTISM IS LAW AND FORCE WITHOUT FREEDOM."

"BARBARISM IS FORCE WITHOUT FREEDOM AND LAW."

"IT IS OF GREAT CONSEQUENCE TO HAVE
PREVIOUSLY DETERMINED THE CONCEPT
THAT ONE WANTS TO ELUCIDATE THROUGH
OBSERVATION BEFORE QUESTIONING
EXPERIENCE ABOUT IT; FOR ONE FINDS IN
EXPERIENCE WHAT ONE NEEDS ONLY IF
ONE KNOWS IN ADVANCE WHAT TO LOOK
FOR."

"REPUBLICANISM IS FORCE WITH FREEDOM
AND LAW."

"IF ADVERSITY AND HOPELESS GRIEF HAVE
QUITE TAKEN AWAY THE TASTE FOR LIFE; IF
AN UNFORTUNATE MAN, STRONG OF SOUL
AND MORE INDIGNANT ABOUT HIS FATE
THAN DESPONDENT OR DEJECTED, WISHES
FOR DEATH AND YET PRESERVES HIS LIFE
WITHOUT LOVING IT, NOT FROM
INCLINATION OR FEAR BUT FROM DUTY,
THEN HIS MAXIM HAS MORAL CONTENT."

"DEFICIENCY IN JUDGEMENT IS PROPERLY THAT WHICH IS CALLED STUPIDITY; AND FOR SUCH A FAILING WE KNOW NO REMEDY. A DULL OR NARROW-MINDED PERSON, TO WHOM NOTHING IS WANTING BUT A PROPER DEGREE OF UNDERSTANDING, MAY BE IMPROVED BY TUITION, EVEN SO FAR AS TO DESERVE THE EPITHET OF LEARNING. BUT AS SUCH PERSONS FREQUENTLY LABOUR UNDER A DEFICIENCY IN THE FACULTY OF JUDGEMENT, IT IS NOT UNCOMMON TO FIND MEN EXTREMELY LEARNED WHO IN THE APPLICATION OF THEIR SCIENCE BETRAY A LAMENTABLE DEGREE THIS IRREMEDIABLE WANT."

"FROM SUCH CROOKED WOOD AS THAT WHICH MAN IS MADE OF, NOTHING STRAIGHT CAN BE FASHIONED."

"WAR SEEMS TO BE INGRAINED IN HUMAN NATURE, AND EVEN TO BE REGARDED AS SOMETHING NOBLE TO WHICH MAN IS INSPIRED BY HIS LOVE OF HONOUR, WITHOUT SELFISH MOTIVES."

"...WHEN HE PUTS A THING ON A PEDESTAL AND CALLS IT BEAUTIFUL, HE DEMANDS THE SAME DELIGHT FROM OTHERS. HE JUDGES NOT MERELY FOR HIMSELF, BUT FOR ALL MEN, AND THEN SPEAKS OF BEAUTY AS IF IT WERE THE PROPERTY OF THINGS."

"NOTHING CAN POSSIBLY BE CONCEIVED IN THE WORLD, OR EVEN OUT OF IT, WHICH CAN BE CALLED GOOD, WITHOUT QUALIFICATION, EXCEPT A GOOD WILL."

"LAUGHTER IS AN AFFECT RESULTING FROM THE SUDDEN TRANSFORMATION OF A HEIGHTENED EXPECTATION INTO NOTHING."

"HE WHO WOULD KNOW THE WORLD MUST FIRST MANUFACTURE IT."

"EVERY BEGINNING IS IN TIME, AND EVERY LIMIT OF EXTENSION IN SPACE. SPACE AND TIME, HOWEVER, EXIST IN THE WORLD OF SENSE ONLY. HENCE PHENOMENA ARE ONLY LIMITED IN THE WORLD CONDITIONALLY, THE WORLD ITSELF, HOWEVER, IS LIMITED NEITHER CONDITIONALLY NOR UNCONDITIONALLY."

RENÉ DESCARTES

ené Descartes was a French philosopher born in 1596, in Touraine in France. He is widely regarded as one of the founders of modern philosophy and had a lot of ground-breaking ideas. In fact, his famous theory "Cogito, ergo sum" or "I think, therefore I am" is a big part in his earning of the nickname: 'the father of modern philosophy'.

Growing up with his great-uncle and grandmother, in 1616, after graduating from the University of Poitiers with a Baccalaureate and License in canon and civil law, he moved to Paris. Descartes spent the years from 1619-1628 travelling Europe. This was due to his resolve to find knowledge from his own experience and from 'the great book of the world'. In conjunction with this, he entirely abandoned 'the study of letters'. Travelling around Europe allowed him to broaden his horizons and experiences as he sought to do, meeting all types of people from a variety of cultures and origins. He would reflect deeply on everything that came his way, to derive value from it.

Later in his life, René Descartes encountered a fierce controversy with the Calvinist theologian Gisbertus Voetius which would continue for the rest of his life. Descartes made a plea for religious tolerance and the rights of man in his *Letter to Voetius,* claiming to write on behalf of Turks (Muslims, atheists and infidels among them) as well as Christians that because Protestants and Catholics worship the same God, both can hope to go to Heaven. When the controversy became intense, Descartes was forced to seek protection.

In 1640, his daughter Francine died of scarlet fever aged five. Speaking on the death, Descartes said he did not believe one must refrain from tears to prove himself a man.

Descartes arranged to give lessons to Queen Christina of Sweden thrice a week. The queen then revealed that the only times she was available would be 5am, and this also meant Descartes staying in her cold and draughty castle. As a result, he caught pneumonia and passed away in February 1650.

I Think, Therefore I Am

René Descartes' most known teaching, *cogito ergo sum* - is proof that we exist. If you ask someone to prove that 2 + 2 is 4, or that you are not indeed dreaming, it's hard to do. Therefore, Descartes concluded that if he doubted, then someone or something must be doing the doubting, thus existing.

Deductive Reasoning

While in Bohemia, he devised a universal method of deductive reasoning, based on mathematics but applicable to all the sciences. It goes as follows:

1. Accept nothing as true that is not self-evident.
2. Divide problems into parts.
3. Solve problems by proceeding from simple to complex.
4. Recheck the reasoning.

This is, of course, still the method used today.

Dualism

This is the thesis that the mind and the body are distinct and there are two kinds of substance: mind and matter. The physical things that are spatially extended are called res extensa, which is what bodies and objects are made of. The mental things like thoughts and ideas which take up no physical space are called res cognita, which is what minds are made of. The natures of the two are completely different, which means one can exist without the other. In this theory, the brain and the mind are not the same things - the brain is the connection between the body and the mind as a physical changeable thing, whereas the mind is whole and indivisible, so losing a limb does not affect the mind. In conjunction with 'I think, therefore I am', the existence of physical things can be questioned but the mind cannot be, as questioning it in itself proves its existence.

5 Facts About Descartes

1. Descartes' finding of 'I think, therefore I am' came to him when on a cold day, he sat inside a stove and spent the whole day meditating inside of it.
2. Cartesian graphs are named after Descartes,

who invented the coordinate system for mathematics.

3. His *Discourses on Method* was one of the first modern philosophical works to not be published in Latin (it was written in French). He said this was so all with good sense, could read it and learn to think for themselves.

4. A lot of his time travelling was spent in the Dutch Republic, as he thought they would be very materialistic and too invested in earning money to concern themselves in the business of a free thinker. The Dutch turned out to be not as materialistic as he'd hoped, and he had to move 24 times to stay ahead of spies and government agents.

5. Once, some friends came to his house in the morning and were shocked to find him in bed at 11 o'clock. They laughed as they asked why he had not risen earlier, to which Descartes laughed back at them for prioritising often nonsensical practical tasks over pure, quiet reflection in bed.

116 RENÉ DESCARTES QUOTES

"DIVIDE EACH DIFFICULTY INTO AS MANY PARTS AS IS FEASIBLE AND NECESSARY TO RESOLVE IT."

"IT IS NOT ENOUGH TO HAVE A GOOD MIND; THE MAIN THING IS TO USE IT WELL."

"COMMON SENSE IS THE MOST FAIRLY DISTRIBUTED THING IN THE WORLD, FOR EACH ONE THINKS HE IS SO WELL-ENDOWED WITH IT THAT EVEN THOSE WHO ARE HARDEST TO SATISFY IN ALL OTHER MATTERS ARE NOT IN THE HABIT OF DESIRING MORE OF IT THAN THEY ALREADY HAVE."

"THE SENSES DECEIVE FROM TIME TO TIME, AND IT IS PRUDENT NEVER TO TRUST WHOLLY THOSE WHO HAVE DECEIVED US EVEN ONCE."

"IF YOU WOULD BE A REAL SEEKER AFTER TRUTH, IT IS NECESSARY THAT AT LEAST ONCE IN YOUR LIFE YOU DOUBT, AS FAR AS POSSIBLE, ALL THINGS."

"EXCEPT OUR OWN THOUGHTS, THERE IS NOTHING ABSOLUTELY IN OUR POWER."

"ONE CANNOT CONCEIVE ANYTHING SO STRANGE AND SO IMPLAUSIBLE THAT IT HAS NOT ALREADY BEEN SAID BY ONE PHILOSOPHER OR ANOTHER."

"PERFECT NUMBERS LIKE PERFECT MEN ARE VERY RARE."

"I HOPE THAT POSTERITY WILL JUDGE ME KINDLY, NOT ONLY AS TO THE THINGS WHICH I HAVE EXPLAINED, BUT ALSO TO THOSE WHICH I HAVE INTENTIONALLY OMITTED SO AS TO LEAVE TO OTHERS THE PLEASURE OF DISCOVERY."

"WHEN IT IS NOT IN OUR POWER TO
FOLLOW WHAT IS TRUE, WE OUGHT TO
FOLLOW WHAT IS MOST PROBABLE."

"I AM ACCUSTOMED TO SLEEP AND IN MY
DREAMS TO IMAGINE THE SAME THINGS
THAT LUNATICS IMAGINE WHEN AWAKE."

"THE FIRST PRECEPT WAS NEVER TO ACCEPT
A THING AS TRUE UNTIL I KNEW IT AS SUCH
WITHOUT A SINGLE DOUBT."

"A STATE IS BETTER GOVERNED WHICH HAS
FEW LAWS, AND THOSE LAWS ARE STRICTLY
OBSERVED."

"I AM INDEED AMAZED WHEN I CONSIDER
HOW WEAK MY MIND IS AND HOW PRONE
TO ERROR."

"WHENEVER ANYONE HAS OFFENDED ME, I
TRY TO RAISE MY SOUL SO HIGH THAT THE
OFFENCE CANNOT REACH IT."

"THE GREATEST MINDS ARE CAPABLE OF THE GREATEST VICES AS WELL AS OF THE GREATEST VIRTUES."

"ILLUSORY JOY IS OFTEN WORTH MORE THAN GENUINE SORROW."

"AN OPTIMIST MAY SEE A LIGHT WHERE THERE IS NONE, BUT WHY MUST THE PESSIMIST ALWAYS RUN TO BLOW IT OUT?"

"TRAVELLING IS ALMOST LIKE TALKING WITH THOSE OF OTHER CENTURIES."

"THE TWO OPERATIONS OF OUR UNDERSTANDING, INTUITION AND DEDUCTION, ON WHICH ALONE WE HAVE SAID WE MUST RELY ON THE ACQUISITION OF KNOWLEDGE."

"IN ORDER TO IMPROVE THE MIND, WE OUGHT LESS TO LEARN, THAN TO CONTEMPLATE."

"EACH PROBLEM THAT I SOLVED BECAME A RULE, WHICH SERVED AFTERWARDS TO SOLVE OTHER PROBLEMS."

"DUBITO ERGO COGITO; COGITO ERGO SUM."

"THE LONG CONCATENATIONS OF SIMPLE AND EASY REASONING WHICH GEOMETRICIANS USE IN ACHIEVING THEIR MOST DIFFICULT DEMONSTRATIONS GAVE ME OCCASION TO IMAGINE THAT ALL MATTERS WHICH MAY ENTER THE HUMAN MIND WERE INTERRELATED IN THE SAME FASHION."

"THE READING OF ALL GOOD BOOKS IS INDEED LIKE A CONVERSATION WITH THE NOBLEST MEN OF PAST CENTURIES WHO WERE THE AUTHORS OF THEM, NAY A CAREFULLY STUDIED CONVERSATION, IN WHICH THEY REVEAL TO US NONE BUT THE BEST OF THEIR THOUGHTS."

"GOOD SENSE IS, OF ALL THINGS AMONG MEN, THE MOST EQUALLY DISTRIBUTED; FOR EVERYONE THINKS HIMSELF SO ABUNDANTLY PROVIDED WITH IT, THAT EVEN THOSE WHO ARE THE MOST DIFFICULT TO SATISFY IN EVERYTHING ELSE, DO NOT USUALLY DESIRE MORE."

"BUT IN MY OPINION, ALL THINGS IN NATURE OCCUR MATHEMATICALLY."

"BECAUSE REASON...IS THE ONLY THING THAT MAKES US MEN, AND DISTINGUISHES US FROM THE BEASTS, I WOULD PREFER TO BELIEVE THAT IT EXISTS, IN ITS ENTIRETY, IN EACH OF US..."

"THE RAINBOW IS SUCH A REMARKABLE PHENOMENON OF NATURE, AND ITS CAUSE HAS BEEN SO METICULOUSLY SOUGHT AFTER BY INQUIRING MINDS THROUGHOUT THE AGES, THAT I COULD NOT CHOOSE A MORE APPROPRIATE SUBJECT FOR DEMONSTRATING HOW, WITH THE METHOD I AM USING, WE CAN ARRIVE AT KNOWLEDGE NOT POSSESSED AT ALL BY THOSE WHOSE WRITINGS ARE AVAILABLE TO US."

"ARCHIMEDES, THAT HE MIGHT TRANSPORT THE ENTIRE GLOBE ... DEMANDED ONLY A POINT THAT WAS FIRM AND IMMOVABLE; SO ALSO, I SHALL BE ENTITLED TO ENTERTAIN THE HIGHEST EXPECTATIONS, IF I AM FORTUNATE ENOUGH TO DISCOVER ONLY ONE THING THAT IS CERTAIN AND INDUBITABLE."

"IT IS BEST NOT TO GO ON A GREAT QUEST FOR TRUTH, IT WILL ONLY MAKE YOU MISERABLE."

"MY THIRD MAXIM WAS TO TRY ALWAYS TO CONQUER MYSELF RATHER THAN FORTUNE, AND TO CHANGE MY DESIRES RATHER THAN THE ORDER OF THE WORLD, AND GENERALLY TO ACCUSTOM MYSELF TO BELIEVING THAT THERE IS NOTHING ENTIRELY IN OUR POWER EXCEPT OUR THOUGHTS, SO THAT AFTER WE HAVE DONE OUR BEST REGARDING THINGS EXTERNAL TO US, EVERYTHING IN WHICH WE DO NOT SUCCEED IS FOR US ABSOLUTELY IMPOSSIBLE."

"WE CALL INFINITE THAT THING WHOSE LIMITS WE HAVE NOT PERCEIVED, AND SO BY THAT WORD WE DO NOT SIGNIFY WHAT WE UNDERSTAND ABOUT A THING, BUT RATHER WHAT WE DO NOT UNDERSTAND."

"I SHOULD CONSIDER THAT I KNOW NOTHING ABOUT PHYSICS IF I WERE ABLE TO EXPLAIN ONLY HOW THINGS MIGHT BE, AND WERE UNABLE TO DEMONSTRATE THAT THEY COULD NOT BE OTHERWISE."

"INSTEAD I OUGHT TO BE GRATEFUL TO HIM WHO NEVER OWED ME ANYTHING FOR HAVING BEEN SO GENEROUS TO ME, RATHER THAN THINK THAT HE DEPRIVED ME OF THOSE THINGS OR HAS TAKEN AWAY FROM ME WHATEVER HE DID NOT GIVE ME."

"YOUR JOY IS YOUR SORROW UNMASKED. AND THE SELF-SAME WELL FROM WHICH YOUR LAUGHTER RISES WAS OFTEN-TIMES FILLED WITH YOUR TEARS."

"I DID NOT IMITATE THE SKEPTICS WHO DOUBT ONLY FOR DOUBTING'S SAKE, AND PRETEND TO BE ALWAYS UNDECIDED; ON THE CONTRARY, MY WHOLE INTENTION WAS TO ARRIVE AT A CERTAINTY, AND TO DIG AWAY THE DRIFT AND THE SAND UNTIL I REACHED THE ROCK OR THE CLAY BENEATH."

"I CONCLUDED THAT I MIGHT TAKE AS A GENERAL RULE THE PRINCIPLE THAT ALL THINGS WHICH WE VERY CLEARLY AND OBVIOUSLY CONCEIVE ARE TRUE: ONLY OBSERVING, HOWEVER, THAT THERE IS SOME DIFFICULTY IN RIGHTLY DETERMINING THE OBJECTS WHICH WE DISTINCTLY CONCEIVE."

"SO BLIND IS THE CURIOSITY BY WHICH MORTALS ARE POSSESSED, THAT THEY OFTEN CONDUCT THEIR MINDS ALONG UNEXPLORED ROUTES, HAVING NO REASON TO HOPE FOR SUCCESS, BUT MERELY BEING WILLING TO RISK THE EXPERIMENT OF FINDING WHETHER THE TRUTH THEY SEEK LIES THERE."

"NEITHER DIVINE GRACE NOR NATURAL KNOWLEDGE EVER DIMINISHES FREEDOM."

"SENSATIONS ARE NOTHING BUT CONFUSED MODES OF THINKING."

"WHEN WRITING ABOUT TRANSCENDENTAL ISSUES, BE TRANSCENDENTALLY CLEAR."

"IT IS CONTRARY TO REASONING TO SAY THAT THERE IS A VACUUM OR SPACE IN WHICH THERE IS ABSOLUTELY NOTHING."

"THERE IS A DIFFERENCE BETWEEN HAPPINESS, THE SUPREME GOOD, AND THE FINAL END OR GOAL TOWARD WHICH OUR ACTIONS OUGHT TO TEND. FOR HAPPINESS IS NOT THE SUPREME GOOD, BUT PRESUPPOSES IT, BEING THE CONTENTMENT OR SATISFACTION OF THE MIND WHICH RESULTS FROM POSSESSING IT."

"FOR HOW DO WE KNOW THAT THE THOUGHTS WHICH OCCUR IN DREAMING ARE FALSE RATHER THAN THOSE OTHERS WHICH WE EXPERIENCE WHEN AWAKE, SINCE THE FORMER ARE OFTEN NOT LESS VIVID AND DISTINCT THAN THE LATTER?"

"NEITHER THE TRUE NOR THE FALSE ROOTS ARE ALWAYS REAL; SOMETIMES THEY ARE IMAGINARY; THAT IS, WHILE WE CAN ALWAYS IMAGINE AS MANY ROOTS FOR EACH EQUATION AS I HAVE ASSIGNED, YET THERE IS NOT ALWAYS A DEFINITE QUANTITY CORRESPONDING TO EACH ROOT WE HAVE IMAGINED."

"IN THE MATTER OF A DIFFICULT QUESTION IT IS MORE LIKELY THAT THE TRUTH SHOULD HAVE BEEN DISCOVERED BY THE FEW THAN BY THE MANY."

"...IT IS CERTAIN THAT I AM REALLY DISTINCT FROM MY BODY, AND CAN EXIST WITHOUT IT."

"EVEN THE MIND DEPENDS SO MUCH ON TEMPERAMENT AND THE DISPOSITION OF ONE'S BODILY ORGANS THAT, IF IT IS POSSIBLE TO FIND A WAY TO MAKE PEOPLE GENERALLY MORE WISE AND MORE SKILFUL THAN THEY HAVE BEEN IN THE PAST, I BELIEVE THAT WE SHOULD LOOK FOR IT IN MEDICINE. IT IS TRUE THAT MEDICINE AS IT IS CURRENTLY PRACTICED CONTAINS LITTLE OF MUCH USE."

"AND AS IT IS THE MOST GENEROUS SOULS WHO HAVE MOST GRATITUDE, IT IS THOSE WHO HAVE MOST PRIDE, AND WHO ARE MOST BASE AND INFIRM, WHO MOST ALLOW THEMSELVES TO BE CARRIED AWAY BY ANGER AND HATRED."

"THE NATURE OF MATTER, OR BODY CONSIDERED IN GENERAL, CONSISTS NOT IN ITS BEING SOMETHING WHICH IS HARD OR HEAVY OR COLOURED, OR WHICH AFFECTS THE SENSES IN ANY WAY, BUT SIMPLY IN ITS BEING SOMETHING WHICH IS EXTENDED IN LENGTH, BREADTH AND DEPTH."

"HENCE REASON ALSO DEMANDS THAT, SINCE OUR THOUGHTS CANNOT ALL BE TRUE BECAUSE WE ARE NOT WHOLLY PERFECT, WHAT TRUTH THEY DO POSSESS MUST INEVITABLY BE FOUND IN THE THOUGHTS WE HAVE WHEN AWAKE, RATHER THAN IN OUR DREAMS."

"THERE IS NOTHING SO FAR REMOVED FROM US TO BE BEYOND OUR REACH, OR SO FAR HIDDEN THAT WE CANNOT DISCOVER IT."

"THE PRINCIPAL USE OF PRUDENCE, OF SELF-CONTROL, IS THAT IT TEACHES US TO BE MASTERS OF OUR PASSIONS, AND TO SO CONTROL AND GUIDE THEM THAT THE EVILS WHICH THEY CAUSE ARE QUITE BEARABLE, AND THAT WE EVEN DERIVE JOY FROM THEM ALL."

"THESE LONG CHAINS OF PERFECTLY SIMPLE AND EASY REASONINGS BY MEANS OF WHICH GEOMETERS ARE ACCUSTOMED TO CARRY OUT THEIR MOST DIFFICULT DEMONSTRATIONS HAD LED ME TO FANCY THAT EVERYTHING THAT CAN FALL UNDER HUMAN KNOWLEDGE FORMS A SIMILAR SEQUENCE; AND THAT SO LONG AS WE AVOID ACCEPTING AS TRUE WHAT IS NOT SO, AND ALWAYS PRESERVE THE RIGHT ORDER OF DEDUCTION OF ONE THING FROM ANOTHER, THERE CAN BE NOTHING TOO REMOTE TO BE REACHED IN THE END, OR TO WELL HIDDEN TO BE DISCOVERED."

"I ACCEPT NO PRINCIPLES OF PHYSICS WHICH ARE NOT ALSO ACCEPTED IN MATHEMATICS."

"THE ENTIRE METHOD CONSISTS IN THE ORDER AND ARRANGEMENT OF THE THINGS TO WHICH THE MIND'S EYE MUST TURN SO THAT WE CAN DISCOVER SOME TRUTH."

71

"THERE IS A GREAT DIFFERENCE BETWEEN MIND AND BODY INSOMUCH AS BODY IS BY NATURE ALWAYS DIVISIBLE, AND THE MIND IS ENTIRELY INDIVISIBLE."

"THERE IS NOTHING MORE ANCIENT THAN THE TRUTH."

"ALTHOUGH MY KNOWLEDGE GROWS MORE AND MORE, NEVERTHELESS I DO NOT FOR THAT REASON BELIEVE THAT IT CAN EVER BE ACTUALLY INFINITE, SINCE IT CAN NEVER REACH A POINT SO HIGH THAT IT WILL BE UNABLE TO ATTAIN ANY GREATER INCREASE."

"I AM A THING THAT THINKS: THAT IS, A THING THAT DOUBTS, AFFIRMS, DENIES, UNDERSTANDS A FEW THINGS, IS IGNORANT OF MANY THINGS, IS WILLING, IS UNWILLING, AND ALSO WHICH IMAGINES AND HAS SENSORY PERCEPTIONS."

"WHEN I CONSIDER THIS CAREFULLY, I FIND NOT A SINGLE PROPERTY WHICH WITH CERTAINTY SEPARATES THE WAKING STATE FROM THE DREAM. HOW CAN YOU BE CERTAIN THAT YOUR WHOLE LIFE IS NOT A DREAM?"

"SOME YEARS AGO I WAS STRUCK BY THE LARGE NUMBER OF FALSEHOODS THAT I HAD ACCEPTED AS TRUE IN MY CHILDHOOD, AND BY THE HIGHLY DOUBTFUL NATURE OF THE WHOLE EDIFICE THAT I HAD SUBSEQUENTLY BASED ON THEM. I REALISED THAT IT WAS NECESSARY, ONCE IN THE COURSE OF MY LIFE, TO DEMOLISH EVERYTHING COMPLETELY AND START AGAIN RIGHT FROM THE FOUNDATIONS IF I WANTED TO ESTABLISH ANYTHING AT ALL IN THE SCIENCES THAT WAS STABLE AND LIKELY TO LAST."

"NOW THEREFORE, THAT MY MIND IS FREE FROM ALL CARES, AND THAT I HAVE OBTAINED FOR MYSELF ASSURED LEISURE IN PEACEFUL SOLITUDE, I SHALL APPLY MYSELF SERIOUSLY AND FREELY TO THE GENERAL DESTRUCTION OF ALL MY FORMER OPINIONS."

"LET WHOEVER CAN DO SO DECEIVE ME, HE WILL NEVER BRING IT ABOUT THAT I AM NOTHING, SO LONG AS I CONTINUE TO THINK I AM SOMETHING."

"I SUPPOSE THEREFORE THAT ALL THINGS I SEE ARE ILLUSIONS; I BELIEVE THAT NOTHING HAS EVER EXISTED OF EVERYTHING MY LYING MEMORY TELLS ME. I THINK I HAVE NO SENSES. I BELIEVE THAT BODY, SHAPE, EXTENSION, MOTION, LOCATION ARE FUNCTIONS. WHAT IS THERE THEN THAT CAN BE TAKEN AS TRUE? PERHAPS ONLY THIS ONE THING, THAT NOTHING AT ALL IS CERTAIN."

"BUT I CANNOT FORGET THAT, AT OTHER TIMES I HAVE BEEN DECEIVED IN SLEEP BY SIMILAR ILLUSIONS; AND, ATTENTIVELY CONSIDERING THOSE CASES, I PERCEIVE SO CLEARLY THAT THERE EXIST NO CERTAIN MARKS BY WHICH THE STATE OF WAKING CAN EVER BE DISTINGUISHED FROM SLEEP, THAT I FEEL GREATLY ASTONISHED; AND IN AMAZEMENT I ALMOST PERSUADE MYSELF THAT I AM NOW DREAMING."

"IT'S THE FAMILIAR LOVE-HATE SYNDROME OF SEDUCTION: "I DON'T REALLY CARE WHAT IT IS I SAY, I CARE ONLY THAT YOU LIKE IT.""

"IF WE POSSESSED A THOROUGH KNOWLEDGE OF ALL THE PARTS OF THE SEED OF ANY ANIMAL (MAN), WE COULD FROM THAT ALONE, BE REASONS ENTIRELY MATHEMATICAL AND CERTAIN, DEDUCE THE WHOLE CONFORMATION AND FIGURE OF EACH OF ITS MEMBERS, AND, CONVERSELY IF WE KNEW SEVERAL PECULIARITIES OF THIS CONFORMATION, WE WOULD FROM THOSE DEDUCE THE NATURE OF ITS SEED."

"IF I GO FOR THE ALTERNATIVE WHICH IS
FALSE, THEN OBVIOUSLY I SHALL BE IN
ERROR; IF I TAKE THE OTHER SIDE, THEN IT
IS BY... CHANCE THAT I ARRIVE AT THE
TRUTH, AND I SHALL STILL BE AT FAULT....
IN THIS INCORRECT USE OF FREE WILL MAY
BE FOUND THE PRIVATION WHICH
CONSTITUTES THE ESSENCE OF ERROR."

"AND I SHALL ALWAYS HOLD MYSELF MORE
OBLIGED TO THOSE BY WHOSE FAVOUR I
ENJOY UNINTERRUPTED LEISURE THAN TO
ANY WHO MIGHT OFFER ME THE MOST
HONOURABLE POSITIONS IN THE WORLD."

"IT IS TO THE BODY ALONE THAT WE
SHOULD ATTRIBUTE EVERYTHING THAT CAN
BE OBSERVED IN US TO OPPOSE OUR
REASON."

"EVEN IF I WERE TO SUPPOSE THAT I WAS
DREAMING AND WHATEVER I SAW OR
IMAGINED WAS FALSE, YET I COULD NOT
DENY THAT IDEAS WERE TRULY IN MY
MIND."

"THE GREATEST MINDS, AS THEY ARE CAPABLE OF THE HIGHEST EXCELLENCIES, ARE OPEN LIKEWISE TO THE GREATEST ABERRATIONS; AND THOSE WHO TRAVEL VERY SLOWLY MAY YET MAKE FAR GREATER PROGRESS, PROVIDED THEY KEEP ALWAYS TO THE STRAIGHT ROAD, THAN THOSE WHO, WHILE THEY RUN, FORSAKE IT."

"AS I CONSIDERED THE MATTER CAREFULLY IT GRADUALLY CAME TO LIGHT THAT ALL THOSE MATTERS ONLY REFERRED TO MATHEMATICS IN WHICH ORDER AND MEASUREMENTS ARE INVESTIGATED, AND THAT IT MAKES NO DIFFERENCE WHETHER IT BE IN NUMBERS, FIGURES, STARS, SOUNDS OR ANY OTHER OBJECT THAT THE QUESTION OF MEASUREMENT ARISES. I SAW CONSEQUENTLY THAT THERE MUST BE SOME GENERAL SCIENCE TO EXPLAIN THAT ELEMENT AS A WHOLE WHICH GIVES RISE TO PROBLEMS ABOUT ORDER AND MEASUREMENT, RESTRICTED AS THESE ARE TO NO SPECIAL SUBJECT MATTER. THIS, I PERCEIVED, WAS CALLED 'UNIVERSAL MATHEMATICS'."

"I AM THINKING, THEREFORE I EXIST. I WAS A SUBSTANCE WHOSE WHOLE ESSENCE OR NATURE IS SOLELY TO THINK, AND WHICH DOES NOT REQUIRE ANY PLACE, OR DEPEND ON ANY MATERIAL THING, IN ORDER TO EXIST. ACCORDINGLY THIS 'I' - THAT IS, THE SOUL BY WHICH I AM WHAT I AM - IS ENTIRELY DISTINCT FROM THE BODY, AND INDEED IS EASIER TO KNOW THAN THE BODY, AND WOULD NOT FAIL TO BE WHATEVER IT IS, EVEN IF THE BODY DID NOT EXIST."

"GIVE ME EXTENSION AND MOTION AND I WILL CONSTRUCT THE UNIVERSE."

"BE THAT AS IT MAY, THERE IS FIXED IN MY MIND A CERTAIN OPINION OF LONG STANDING, NAMELY THAT THERE EXISTS A GOD WHO IS ABLE TO DO ANYTHING AND BY WHOM I, SUCH AS I AM, HAVE BEEN CREATED. HOW DO I KNOW THAT HE DID NOT BRING IT ABOUT THAT THERE IS NO EARTH AT ALL, NO HEAVENS, NO EXTENDED THING, NO SHAPE, NO SIZE, NO PLACE, AND YET BRINGING IT ABOUT THAT ALL THESE THINGS APPEAR TO ME TO EXIST PRECISELY AS THEY DO NOW?"

"THE MIND EFFORTLESSLY AND AUTOMATICALLY TAKES IN NEW IDEAS, WHICH REMAIN IN LIMBO UNTIL VERIFIED OR REJECTED BY CONSCIOUS, RATIONAL ANALYSIS."

"BAD BOOKS ENGENDER BAD HABITS, BUT BAD HABITS ENGENDER GOOD BOOKS."

"HERE I BEG YOU TO OBSERVE IN PASSING THAT THE SCRUPLES THAT PREVENTED ANCIENT WRITERS FROM USING ARITHMETICAL TERMS IN GEOMETRY, AND WHICH CAN ONLY BE A CONSEQUENCE OF THEIR INABILITY TO PERCEIVE CLEARLY THE RELATION BETWEEN THESE TWO SUBJECTS, INTRODUCED MUCH OBSCURITY AND CONFUSION INTO THEIR EXPLANATIONS."

"WHAT THEN IS THE SOURCE OF MY ERRORS? THEY ARE OWING SIMPLY TO THE FACT THAT, SINCE THE WILL EXTENDS FURTHER THAN THE INTELLECT, I DO NOT CONTAIN THE WILL WITHIN THE SAME BOUNDARIES; RATHER, I ALSO EXTEND IT TO THINGS I DO NOT UNDERSTAND. BECAUSE THE WILL IS INDIFFERENT IN REGARD TO SUCH MATTERS, IT EASILY TURNS AWAY FROM THE TRUE AND THE GOOD; AND IN THIS WAY I AM DECEIVED AND I SIN."

"TO LIVE WITHOUT PHILOSOPHISING IS IN TRUTH THE SAME AS KEEPING THE EYES CLOSED WITHOUT ATTEMPTING TO OPEN THEM."

"IN PHILOSOPHY, WHEN WE MAKE USE OF FALSE PRINCIPLES, WE DEPART THE FARTHER FROM THE KNOWLEDGE OF TRUTH AND WISDOM EXACTLY IN PROPORTION TO THE CARE WITH WHICH WE CULTIVATE THEM, AND APPLY OURSELVES TO THE DEDUCTION OF DIVERSE CONSEQUENCES FROM THEM, THINKING THAT WE ARE PHILOSOPHISING WELL, WHILE WE ARE ONLY DEPARTING THE FARTHER FROM THE TRUTH; FROM WHICH IT MUST BE INFERRED THAT THEY WHO HAVE LEARNED THE LEAST OF ALL THAT HAS BEEN HITHERTO DISTINGUISHED BY THE NAME OF PHILOSOPHY ARE THE MOST FITTED FOR THE APPREHENSION OF TRUTH."

"HOW DO WE KNOW THAT ANYTHING REALLY EXISTS, THAT ANYTHING IS REALLY THE WAY IT SEEMS TO US THROUGH OUR SENSES?"

"REASON IS NOTHING WITHOUT IMAGINATION."

"IN GOD THERE IS AN INFINITUDE OF THINGS WHICH I CANNOT COMPREHEND, NOR POSSIBLY EVEN REACH IN ANY WAY BY THOUGHT; FOR IT IS THE NATURE OF THE INFINITE THAT MY NATURE, WHICH IS FINITE AND LIMITED, SHOULD NOT COMPREHEND IT."

"IT MUST NOT BE THOUGHT THAT IT IS EVER POSSIBLE TO REACH THE INTERIOR EARTH BY ANY PERSEVERANCE IN MINING: BOTH BECAUSE THE EXTERIOR EARTH IS TOO THICK, IN COMPARISON WITH HUMAN STRENGTH; AND ESPECIALLY BECAUSE OF THE INTERMEDIATE WATERS, WHICH WOULD GUSH FORTH WITH GREATER IMPETUS, THE DEEPER THE PLACE IN WHICH THEIR VEINS WERE FIRST OPENED; AND WHICH WOULD DROWN ALL MINERS."

"SCIENCE IS PRACTICAL PHILOSOPHY."

"EVERYTHING IS SELF-EVIDENT."

"FEW LOOK FOR TRUTH; MANY PROWL
ABOUT FOR A REPUTATION OF PROFUNDITY
BY ARROGANTLY CHALLENGING WHICHEVER
ARGUMENTS ARE THE BEST."

"EVEN THOSE WHO HAVE THE WEAKEST
SOULS COULD ACQUIRE ABSOLUTE MASTERY
OVER ALL THEIR PASSIONS IF WE EMPLOYED
SUFFICIENT INGENUITY IN TRAINING AND
GUIDING THEM."

"INTUITION IS THE UNDOUBTING
CONCEPTION OF A PURE AND ATTENTIVE
MIND, WHICH ARISES FROM THE LIGHT OF
REASON ALONE, AND IS MORE CERTAIN
THAN DEDUCTION."

"DOUBT IS THE ORIGIN OF WISDOM."

"AT LAST I WILL DEVOTE MYSELF SINCERELY
AND WITHOUT RESERVATION TO THE
GENERAL DEMOLITION OF MY OPINIONS."

"SO FAR, I HAVE BEEN A SPECTATOR IN THIS THEATRE WHICH IS THE WORLD, BUT I AM NOW ABOUT TO MOUNT THE STAGE, AND I COME FORWARD MASKED."

"JUST AS WE BELIEVE BY FAITH THAT THE GREATEST HAPPINESS OF THE NEXT LIFE CONSISTS SIMPLY IN THE CONTEMPLATION OF THIS DIVINE MAJESTY, LIKEWISE WE EXPERIENCE THAT WE DERIVE THE GREATEST JOY OF WHICH WE ARE CAPABLE IN THIS LIFE FROM THE SAME CONTEMPLATION, EVEN THOUGH IT IS MUCH LESS PERFECT."

"I HAVE CONCLUDED THE EVIDENT EXISTENCE OF GOD, AND THAT MY EXISTENCE DEPENDS ENTIRELY ON GOD IN ALL THE MOMENTS OF MY LIFE, THAT I DO NOT THINK THAT THE HUMAN SPIRIT MAY KNOW ANYTHING WITH GREATER EVIDENCE AND CERTITUDE."

"EVERY MAN IS INDEED BOUND TO DO WHAT HE CAN TO PROMOTE THE GOOD OF OTHERS, AND A MAN WHO IS OF NO USE TO ANYONE IS STRICTLY WORTHLESS."

"IF IT IS NOT IN MY POWER TO ARRIVE AT THE KNOWLEDGE OF ANY TRUTH, I MAY AT LEAST DO WHAT IS IN MY POWER, NAMELY, SUSPEND JUDGEMENT."

"INTUITIVE KNOWLEDGE IS AN ILLUMINATION OF THE SOUL, WHEREBY IT BEHOLDS IN THE LIGHT OF GOD THOSE THINGS WHICH IT PLEASES HIM TO REVEAL TO US BY A DIRECT IMPRESSION OF DIVINE CLEARNESS."

"... REGARD THIS BODY AS A MACHINE WHICH, HAVING BEEN MADE BY THE HAND OF GOD, IS INCOMPARABLY BETTER ORDERED THAN ANY MACHINE THAT CAN BE DEVISED BY MAN, AND CONTAINS IN ITSELF MOVEMENTS MORE WONDERFUL THAN THOSE IN ANY MACHINE. ... IT IS FOR ALL PRACTICAL PURPOSES IMPOSSIBLE FOR A MACHINE TO HAVE ENOUGH ORGANS TO MAKE IT ACT IN ALL THE CONTINGENCIES OF LIFE IN THE WAY IN WHICH OUR REASON MAKES US ACT."

"HUMAN WISDOM REMAINS ALWAYS ONE AND THE SAME ALTHOUGH APPLIED TO THE MOST DIVERSE OBJECTS AND IT IS NO MORE CHANGED BY THEIR DIVERSITY THAN THE SUNSHINE IS CHANGED BY THE VARIETY OF OBJECTS WHICH IT ILLUMINATES."

"TRUTHS ARE MORE LIKELY TO BE DISCOVERED BY ONE MAN THAN BY A NATION."

"WONDER IS THE FIRST OF ALL THE PASSIONS."

"THIS RESULT COULD HAVE BEEN ACHIEVED EITHER BY HIS ENDOWING MY INTELLECT WITH A CLEAR AND DISTINCT PERCEPTION OF EVERYTHING ABOUT WHICH I WOULD EVER DELIBERATE, OR SIMPLY BY IMPRESSING THE FOLLOWING RULE SO FIRMLY UPON MY MEMORY THAT I COULD NEVER FORGET IT: I SHOULD NEVER JUDGE ANYTHING THAT I DO NOT CLEARLY AND DISTINCTLY UNDERSTAND."

"YOU JUST KEEP PUSHING. YOU JUST KEEP PUSHING. I MADE EVERY MISTAKE THAT COULD BE MADE. BUT I JUST KEPT PUSHING."

"WE NEVER UNDERSTAND A THING SO WELL AND MAKE IT OUR OWN, AS WHEN WE HAVE DISCOVERED IT FOR OURSELVES."

"I KNOW THAT I EXIST; THE QUESTION IS, WHAT IS THIS 'I' THAT 'I' KNOW."

"MATHEMATICS IS A MORE POWERFUL INSTRUMENT OF KNOWLEDGE THAN ANY OTHER THAT HAS BEEN BEQUEATHED TO US BY HUMAN AGENCY."

"SITUATIONS IN LIFE OFTEN PERMIT NO DELAY; AND WHEN WE CANNOT DETERMINE THE COURSE WHICH IS CERTAINLY BEST, WE MUST FOLLOW THE ONE WHICH IS PROBABLY THE BEST. THIS FRAME OF MIND FREED ME ALSO FROM THE REPENTANCE AND REMORSE COMMONLY FELT BY THOSE VACILLATING INDIVIDUALS WHO ARE ALWAYS SEEKING AS WORTHWHILE THINGS WHICH THEY LATER JUDGE TO BE BAD."

"ANY COMMUNITY THAT GETS ITS LAUGHS BY PRETENDING TO BE IDIOTS WILL EVENTUALLY BE FLOODED BY ACTUAL IDIOTS WHO MISTAKENLY BELIEVE THAT THEY'RE IN GOOD COMPANY."

"BUT POSSIBLY I AM SOMETHING MORE THAN I SUPPOSE MYSELF TO BE."

"BEFORE EXAMINING THIS MORE CAREFULLY AND INVESTIGATING ITS CONSEQUENCES, I WANT TO DWELL FOR A MOMENT IN THE CONTEMPLATION OF GOD, TO PONDER HIS ATTRIBUTES IN ME, TO SEE, ADMIRE, AND ADORE THE BEAUTY OF HIS BOUNDLESS LIGHT, INSOFAR AS MY CLOUDED INSIGHT ALLOWS. BELIEVING THAT THE SUPREME HAPPINESS OF THE OTHER LIFE CONSISTS WHOLLY OF THE CONTEMPLATION OF DIVINE GREATNESS, I NOW FIND THAT THROUGH LESS PERFECT CONTEMPLATION OF THE SAME SORT I CAN GAIN THE GREATEST JOY AVAILABLE IN THIS LIFE."

"THE CHIEF CAUSE OF HUMAN ERRORS IS TO BE FOUND IN THE PREJUDICES PICKED UP IN CHILDHOOD."

"WE DO NOT DESCRIBE THE WORLD WE SEE, WE SEE THE WORLD WE DESCRIBE."

"... MORAL CERTAINTY IS CERTAINTY WHICH IS SUFFICIENT TO REGULATE OUR BEHAVIOUR, OR WHICH MEASURES UP TO THE CERTAINTY WE HAVE ON MATTERS RELATING TO THE CONDUCT OF LIFE WHICH WE NEVER NORMALLY DOUBT, THOUGH WE KNOW THAT IT IS POSSIBLE, ABSOLUTELY SPEAKING, THAT THEY MAY BE FALSE."

PLATO

*I*n Athens, around 427 BC, a prodigy known as Plato would be born. Plato would go on to become one of the world's most famous philosophers, with many of his teachings and ideas still being studied in the present day. From a very young age until the point of death, Plato was seen as an outstanding thinker.

Plato was born into a very wealthy family. Throughout his life, he was on a quest to help individuals in society reach a particular state he termed 'Eudaemonia' which can be translated to fulfilment. Plato maintains a virtue-based eudaemonistic conception of ethics. That is to say, happiness or well-being (eudaemonia) is the highest aim of moral thought and conduct, and the virtues (arête: 'excellence') are the requisite skills and dispositions needed to attain it.

Plato was actually a pupil of another famous philosopher, Socrates. Funnily enough, as well as this he was the teacher and mentor of Aristotle.

Plato was a very enthusiastic and passionate soul who loved to write, clearly observable by the 36 books which he managed to create through his life's work.

To name just a few of his well-known works:

- The Apology
- The Republic
- The Meno
- The Law
- The Symposium

These books played a huge role in the way art, ethics, metaphysics, mind, realism were viewed at that time.

Think for Yourself

Plato strongly believed that due to the fact we are free, autonomous beings we should take the time to reflect on our thoughts and ensure we leave ourselves enough time in the day to simply 'think'. He believed that once in a while one should analyse, and evaluate their thoughts. He believed we should challenge our own thoughts, in doing so we can avoid Doxas - popular opinion. Plato hated the idea of having a popular opinion because of its flaw of always glorifying the wrong values.

Plato believed that the only way to fully break out of popular opinion is by practising philosophy and giving yourself time to think, evaluate and rationalise your thoughts, leaving you better able to decide whether that is an opinion you have because it's right or whether that's an opinion you have due to external influences.

End Democracy

Plato believed there were way too many uneducated people who vote, meaning a lot of votes were being cast through irrational logic, which dilutes the power of democracy. If you have someone uneducated about politics and they are going in to vote it diminishes the power that their vote has as it's an uneducated vote, rather than a thought out, logical vote, thus causing the wrong people to always get voted into power.

Few people are properly educated. Therefore Plato believed we must educate the masses. Our goal should be to get to a point where everyone is thinking freely and rationally.

Forms

Plato believed that we lived in a world of forms. The world is split into two separate parts, the physical and the spiritual. The physical is everything that can be seen, measured and observed in the empirical world, but reality goes far beyond the physical world. The spiritual is a place in the realm of forms. Plato believed that everything that we currently observe is just a shadow of the spiritual realm. In addition, things in the spiritual realm were abstract, perfect, unchanging and unaffected by time and space.

In order to be the best version of ourselves or to create the best version of a thing, we must draw great influence from the spiritual realm. He believed that we are able to use the realm of forms to help us get to the closest version of perfect. The forms acted as a template for us to use.

5 Facts About Plato

1. Plato's mother married his uncle when his father died.
2. The Roman emperor at the time, Justinian, considered the academy which was founded by Plato as a threat to Christianity and decided to completely close the school down.
3. Plato was once offered the chance to be a ruler of Athens with 30 other tyrants. He refused the offer.
4. Plato believed that at the centre of love should be admiration. We must look for a partner that has all the features we are missing from ourselves with hopes that they can influence us to be more like them.
5. It is rumoured that Plato was named after his father and his real name is supposedly Aristocles.

95 PLATO QUOTES

"DO NOT TRAIN A CHILD TO LEARN BY FORCE OR HARSHNESS; BUT DIRECT THEM TO IT BY WHAT AMUSES THEIR MINDS, SO THAT YOU MAY BE BETTER ABLE TO DISCOVER WITH ACCURACY THE PECULIAR BENT OF THE GENIUS OF EACH."

"WISE MEN TALK BECAUSE THEY HAVE SOMETHING TO SAY; FOOLS, BECAUSE THEY HAVE TO SAY SOMETHING."

"WE CAN EASILY FORGIVE A CHILD WHO IS AFRAID OF THE DARK; THE REAL TRAGEDY OF LIFE IS WHEN MEN ARE AFRAID OF THE LIGHT."

"THE FIRST AND THE BEST VICTORY IS TO CONQUER SELF."

"THE PENALTY GOOD MEN PAY FOR INDIFFERENCE TO PUBLIC AFFAIRS IS TO BE RULED BY EVIL MEN."

"LOVE IS A SERIOUS MENTAL DISEASE."

"IN POLITICS WE PRESUME THAT EVERYONE WHO KNOWS HOW TO GET VOTES KNOWS HOW TO ADMINISTER A REGION. WHEN WE ARE ILL... WE DO NOT ASK FOR THE HANDSOMEST PHYSICIAN, OR THE MOST ELOQUENT ONE."

"I HAVE GOOD HOPE THAT THERE IS SOMETHING AFTER DEATH."

"WE ARE TWICE ARMED IF WE FIGHT WITH FAITH."

"OPINION IS THE MEDIUM BETWEEN KNOWLEDGE AND IGNORANCE."

"ONLY THE DEAD HAVE SEEN THE END OF WAR."

"THINKING IS THE TALKING OF THE SOUL WITH ITSELF."

"THE BEGINNING IS THE MOST IMPORTANT PART OF THE WORK."

"FOR JUST AS POETS LOVE THEIR OWN WORKS, AND FATHERS THEIR OWN CHILDREN, IN THE SAME WAY THOSE WHO HAVE CREATED A FORTUNE VALUE THEIR MONEY, NOT MERELY FOR ITS USES, LIKE OTHER PERSONS, BUT BECAUSE IT IS THEIR OWN PRODUCTION. THIS MAKES THEM MOREOVER DISAGREEABLE COMPANIONS, BECAUSE THEY WILL PRAISE NOTHING BUT RICHES."

"POETS UTTER GREAT AND WISE THINGS WHICH THEY DO NOT THEMSELVES UNDERSTAND."

"THOSE WHO INTEND ON BECOMING GREAT SHOULD LOVE NEITHER THEMSELVES OR THEIR OWN THINGS, BUT ONLY WHAT IS JUST, WHETHER IT HAPPENS TO BE DONE BY THEMSELVES OR OTHERS."

"A GOOD DECISION IS BASED ON KNOWLEDGE AND NOT ON NUMBERS."

"I HAVE HARDLY EVER KNOWN A MATHEMATICIAN WHO WAS CAPABLE OF REASONING."

"ALL LEARNING HAS AN EMOTIONAL BASE."

"WE OUGHT TO ESTEEM IT OF THE GREATEST IMPORTANCE THAT THE FICTIONS WHICH CHILDREN FIRST HEAR SHOULD BE ADAPTED IN THE MOST PERFECT MANNER TO THE PROMOTION OF VIRTUE."

"HONESTY IS FOR THE MOST PART, LESS PROFITABLE THAN DISHONESTY."

"WISDOM ALONE IS THE SCIENCE OF OTHER SCIENCES."

"NOTHING IN THE AFFAIRS OF MEN IS WORTHY OF GREAT ANXIETY."

"KNOWLEDGE BECOMES EVIL IF THE AIM BE NOT VIRTUOUS."

"ALL THINGS WILL BE PRODUCED IN SUPERIOR QUANTITY AND QUALITY, AND WITH GREATER EASE, WHEN EACH MAN WORKS AT A SINGLE OCCUPATION, IN ACCORDANCE WITH HIS NATURAL GIFTS, AND AT THE RIGHT MOMENT, WITHOUT MEDDLING WITH ANYTHING ELSE."

"THERE MUST ALWAYS REMAIN SOMETHING THAT IS ANTAGONISTIC TO GOOD."

"THESE, THEN, WILL BE SOME OF THE FEATURES OF DEMOCRACY... IT WILL BE, IN ALL LIKELIHOOD, AN AGREEABLE, LAWLESS, PARTI-COLORED COMMONWEALTH, DEALING WITH ALL ALIKE ON A FOOTING OF EQUALITY, WHETHER THEY BE REALLY EQUAL OR NOT."

"POETRY COMES NEARER TO VITAL TRUTH THAN HISTORY."

"HE BEST KEEPS FROM ANGER WHO REMEMBERS THAT GOD IS ALWAYS LOOKING UPON HIM."

"THEY DO CERTAINLY GIVE VERY STRANGE, AND NEWFANGLED, NAMES TO DISEASES."

"IT IS CLEAR TO EVERYONE THAT ASTRONOMY AT ALL EVENTS COMPELS THE SOUL TO LOOK UPWARDS, AND DRAWS IT FROM THE THINGS OF THIS WORLD TO THE OTHER."

"NO-ONE KNOWS WHETHER DEATH, WHICH PEOPLE FEAR TO BE THE GREATEST EVIL, MAY BE THE GREATEST GOOD."

"THERE ARE THREE CLASSES OF MEN; LOVERS OF WISDOM, LOVERS OF HONOR, AND LOVERS OF GAIN."

"MUSIC GIVES A SOUL TO THE UNIVERSE, WINGS TO THE MIND, FLIGHT TO THE IMAGINATION, AND LIFE TO EVERYTHING..."

"NECESSITY IS THE MOTHER OF INVENTION."

"THEY DEEM HIM THEIR WORST ENEMY WHO TELLS THEM THE TRUTH."

"THIS ALONE IS TO BE FEARED: THE CLOSED MIND, THE SLEEPING IMAGINATION, THE DEATH OF SPIRIT."

"THE PEOPLE ALWAYS HAVE SOME CHAMPION WHOM THEY SET OVER THEM AND NURSE INTO GREATNESS. THIS AND NO OTHER IS THE ROOT FROM WHICH A TYRANT SPRINGS; WHEN HE FIRST APPEARS HE IS A PROTECTOR."

"A HOUSE THAT HAS A LIBRARY IN IT HAS A SOUL."

"HOMOSEXUALITY, IS REGARDED AS
SHAMEFUL BY BARBARIANS AND BY THOSE
WHO LIVE UNDER DESPOTIC GOVERNMENTS
JUST AS PHILOSOPHY IS REGARDED AS
SHAMEFUL BY THEM, BECAUSE IT IS
APPARENTLY NOT IN THE INTEREST OF
SUCH RULERS TO HAVE GREAT IDEAS
ENGENDERED IN THEIR SUBJECTS, OR
POWERFUL FRIENDSHIPS OR PASSIONATE
LOVE - ALL OF WHICH HOMOSEXUALITY IS
PARTICULARLY APT TO PRODUCE."

"THE WISEST HAVE THE MOST AUTHORITY."

"DICTATORSHIP NATURALLY ARISES OUT OF
DEMOCRACY, AND THE MOST AGGRAVATED
FORM OF TYRANNY AND SLAVERY OUT OF
THE MOST EXTREME LIBERTY."

"THE MEASURE OF A MAN IS WHAT HE DOES
WITH POWER."

"THE SPIRITUAL EYESIGHT IMPROVES AS
THE PHYSICAL EYESIGHT DECLINES."

"THE MOST VIRTUOUS ARE THOSE WHO
CONTENT THEMSELVES WITH BEING
VIRTUOUS WITHOUT SEEKING TO
APPEAR SO."

"PLEASURE IS THE GREATEST INCENTIVE TO
EVIL."

"YOU CANNOT CONCEIVE THE MANY
WITHOUT THE ONE."

"RHETORIC IS THE ART OF RULING THE
MINDS OF MEN."

"NO WEALTH CAN EVER MAKE A BAD MAN AT
PEACE WITH HIMSELF."

"OF ALL THE ANIMALS, THE BOY IS THE
MOST UNMANAGEABLE."

"IGNORANCE OF ALL THINGS IS AN EVIL
NEITHER TERRIBLE NOR EXCESSIVE, NOR
YET THE GREATEST OF ALL; BUT GREAT
CLEVERNESS AND MUCH LEARNING, IF THEY
ARE ACCOMPANIED BY A BAD TRAINING, ARE
A MUCH GREATER MISFORTUNE."

"DEMOCRACY IS A CHARMING FORM OF
GOVERNMENT, FULL OF VARIETY AND
DISORDER, AND DISPENSING A SORT OF
EQUALITY TO EQUALS AND UNEQUAL ALIKE."

"ARGUMENTS, LIKE MEN, ARE OFTEN
PRETENDERS."

"OLD AGE HAS A GREAT SENSE OF CALM AND
FREEDOM. WHEN THE PASSIONS HAVE
RELAXED THEIR HOLD AND HAVE ESCAPED,
NOT FROM ONE MASTER, BUT FROM MANY."

"STATES ARE AS MEN, THEY GROW OUT OF
HUMAN CHARACTERS."

"WHEN A BEAUTIFUL SOUL HARMONIZES WITH A BEAUTIFUL FORM, AND THE TWO ARE CAST IN ONE MOULD, THAT WILL BE THE FAIREST OF SIGHTS TO HIM WHO HAS THE EYE TO CONTEMPLATE THE VISION."

"KNOWLEDGE WHICH IS ACQUIRED UNDER COMPULSION OBTAINS NO HOLD ON THE MIND."

"MUSIC IS TO THE MIND AS AIR IS TO THE BODY."

"JUSTICE IN THE LIFE AND CONDUCT OF THE STATE IS POSSIBLE ONLY AS FIRST IT RESIDES IN THE HEARTS AND SOULS OF THE CITIZENS."

"THERE ARE FEW PEOPLE SO STUBBORN IN THEIR ATHEISM WHO WHEN DANGER IS PRESSING IN WILL NOT ACKNOWLEDGE THE DIVINE POWER."

"THEN THE LOVER, WHO IS TRUE AND NO COUNTERFEIT, MUST OF NECESSITY BE LOVED BY HIS LOVE."

"MUSIC IS THE MOVEMENT OF SOUND TO REACH THE SOUL FOR THE EDUCATION OF ITS VIRTUE."

"WE OUGHT TO FLY AWAY FROM EARTH TO HEAVEN AS QUICKLY AS WE CAN; AND TO FLY AWAY IS TO BECOME LIKE GOD, AS FAR AS THIS IS POSSIBLE; AND TO BECOME LIKE HIM IS TO BECOME HOLY, JUST, AND WISE."

"HE WHO IS OF A CALM AND HAPPY NATURE WILL HARDLY FEEL THE PRESSURE OF AGE, BUT TO HIM WHO IS OF AN OPPOSITE DISPOSITION YOUTH AND AGE ARE EQUALLY A BURDEN."

"THE SOUL IS PARTLY IN ETERNITY AND PARTLY IN TIME."

"INTEGRITY IS YOUR DESTINY - IT IS THE LIGHT THAT GUIDES YOUR WAY."

"NO ONE EVER TEACHES WELL WHO WANTS TO TEACH, OR GOVERNS WELL WHO WANTS TO GOVERN."

"THE SOULS OF PEOPLE, ON THEIR WAY TO EARTH-LIFE, PASS THROUGH A ROOM FULL OF LIGHTS; EACH TAKES A TAPER - OFTEN ONLY A SPARK - TO GUIDE IT IN THE DIM COUNTRY OF THIS WORLD. BUT SOME SOULS, BY RARE FORTUNE, ARE DETAINED LONGER - HAVE TIME TO GRASP A HANDFUL OF TAPERS, WHICH THEY WEAVE INTO A TORCH. THESE ARE THE TORCH-BEARERS OF HUMANITY - ITS POETS, SEERS AND SAINTS, WHO LEAD AND LIFT THE RACE OUT OF DARKNESS, TOWARD THE LIGHT. THEY ARE THE LAW-GIVERS AND SAVIORS, THE LIGHT-BRINGERS, WAY-SHOWERS AND TRUTH-TELLERS, AND WITHOUT THEM, HUMANITY WOULD LOSE ITS WAY IN THE DARK."

"WE ARE BOUND TO OUR BODIES LIKE AN OYSTER IS TO ITS SHELL."

"SCIENCE IS NOTHING BUT PERCEPTION."

"LET US DESCRIBE THE EDUCATION OF OUR MEN. WHAT THEN IS THE EDUCATION TO BE? PERHAPS WE COULD HARDLY FIND BETTER THAN THAT WHICH THE EXPERIENCE OF THE PAST HAS ALREADY DISCOVERED, WHICH CONSISTS, I BELIEVE, IN GYMNASTICS, FOR THE BODY, AND MUSIC FOR THE MIND."

"EXCESS GENERALLY CAUSES REACTION, AND PRODUCES A CHANGE IN THE OPPOSITE DIRECTION, WHETHER IT BE IN THE SEASONS, OR IN INDIVIDUALS, OR IN GOVERNMENTS."

"LOVE IS THE JOY OF THE GOOD, THE WONDER OF THE WISE, THE AMAZEMENT OF THE GODS."

"THE EXCESSIVE INCREASE OF ANYTHING
CAUSES A REACTION IN THE OPPOSITE
DIRECTION."

"LET NOBODY SPEAK MISCHIEF OF
ANYBODY."

"ANY CITY HOWEVER SMALL, IS IN FACT
DIVIDED INTO TWO, ONE THE CITY OF THE
POOR, THE OTHER OF THE RICH. THESE ARE
AT WAR WITH ONE ANOTHER."

"THOSE WRETCHES WHO NEVER HAVE
EXPERIENCED THE SWEETS OF WISDOM
AND VIRTUE, BUT SPEND ALL THEIR TIME IN
REVELS AND DEBAUCHES, SINK DOWNWARD
DAY AFTER DAY, AND MAKE THEIR WHOLE
LIFE ONE CONTINUED SERIES OF ERRORS.
THEY TASTE NO REAL OR SUBSTANTIAL
PLEASURE; BUT, RESEMBLING SO MANY
BRUTES, WITH EYES ALWAYS FIXED ON THE
EARTH, AND INTENT UPON THEIR LOADEN
TABLES, THEY PAMPER THEMSELVES IN
LUXURY AND EXCESS."

"WHATEVER DECEIVES MEN SEEMS TO PRODUCE A MAGICAL ENCHANTMENT."

"OUR OBJECT IN THE CONSTRUCTION OF THE STATE IS THE GREATEST HAPPINESS OF THE WHOLE, AND NOT THAT OF ANY ONE CLASS."

"BEAUTY OF STYLE AND HARMONY AND GRACE AND GOOD RHYTHM DEPENDS ON SIMPLICITY."

"THE HEAVIEST PENALTY FOR DECIDING TO ENGAGE IN POLITICS IS TO BE RULED BY SOMEONE INFERIOR TO YOURSELF."

"PHILOSOPHY IS AN ELEGANT THING IF ANYONE MODESTLY MEDDLES WITH IT; BUT IF THEY ARE CONVERSANT WITH IT MORE THAN IS BECOMING, IT CORRUPTS THEM."

"THE DEMOCRATIC YOUTH LIVES ALONG DAY BY DAY, GRATIFYING THE DESIRE THAT OCCURS TO HIM, AT ONE TIME DRINKING AND LISTENING TO THE FLUTE, AT ANOTHER DOWNING WATER AND REDUCING, NOW PRACTICING GYMNASTICS, AND AGAIN IDLING AND NEGLECTING EVERYTHING; AND SOMETIMES SPENDING HIS TIME AS THOUGH HE WERE OCCUPIED IN PHILOSOPHY."

"IF THE STUDY OF ALL THESE SCIENCES WHICH WE HAVE ENUMERATED, SHOULD EVER BRING US TO THEIR MUTUAL ASSOCIATION AND RELATIONSHIP, AND TEACH US THE NATURE OF THE TIES WHICH BIND THEM TOGETHER, I BELIEVE THAT THE DILIGENT TREATMENT OF THEM WILL FORWARD THE OBJECTS WHICH WE HAVE IN VIEW, AND THAT THE LABOR, WHICH OTHERWISE WOULD BE FRUITLESS, WILL BE WELL BESTOWED."

"NO TRACE OF SLAVERY OUGHT TO MIX WITH THE STUDIES OF THE FREEBORN MAN. NO STUDY, PURSUED UNDER COMPULSION, REMAINS ROOTED IN THE MEMORY."

"I EXHORT YOU ALSO TO TAKE PART IN THE GREAT COMBAT, WHICH IS THE COMBAT OF LIFE, AND GREATER THAN EVERY OTHER EARTHLY CONFLICT."

"TO THE RULERS OF THE STATE THEN, IF TO ANY, IT BELONGS OF RIGHT TO USE FALSEHOOD, TO DECEIVE EITHER ENEMIES OR THEIR OWN CITIZENS, FOR THE GOOD OF THE STATE: AND NO ONE ELSE MAY MEDDLE WITH THIS PRIVILEGE."

"TOO MUCH ATTENTION TO HEALTH IS A HINDRANCE TO LEARNING, TO INVENTION, AND TO STUDIES OF ANY KIND, FOR WE ARE ALWAYS FEELING SUSPICIOUS SHOOTINGS AND SWIMMINGS IN OUR HEADS, AND WE ARE PRONE TO BLAME STUDIES FROM THEM."

"LET PARENTS BEQUEATH TO THEIR CHILDREN NOT RICHES, BUT THE SPIRIT OF REVERENCE."

"THE MADNESS OF LOVE IS THE GREATEST OF HEAVEN'S BLESSINGS."

"WHEN THE MIND IS THINKING IT IS TALKING TO ITSELF."

"IS IT NOT ALSO TRUE THAT NO PHYSICIAN, IN SO FAR AS HE IS A PHYSICIAN, CONSIDERS OR ENJOINS WHAT IS FOR THE PHYSICIAN'S INTEREST, BUT THAT ALL SEEK THE GOOD OF THEIR PATIENTS? FOR WE HAVE AGREED THAT A PHYSICIAN STRICTLY SO CALLED, IS A RULER OF BODIES, AND NOT A MAKER OF MONEY, HAVE WE NOT?"

"WHEN MEN SPEAK ILL OF THEE, LIVE SO AS NOBODY MAY BELIEVE THEM."

"WEALTH IS WELL KNOWN TO BE A GREAT COMFORTER."

"HEREDITARY HONORS ARE A NOBLE AND A SPLENDID TREASURE TO DESCENDANTS."

SOCRATES

*S*ocrates was, and might still be one of the most influential philosophers in western society, as the first moral philosopher of the western ethical tradition of thought.

Socrates was born in Athens in 469 BC. During this time, many changes were occurring including a shift to a more democratic system. Before Socrates would go on to become a philosopher he started off working as a shoe welter and also served in the military as a soldier.

Socrates would famously travel various regions, speaking up in conversations and confronting people about the beliefs which they had held up to this point because it's important to challenge oneself and to understand that we know nothing at all.

Socrates was a very influential teacher with many young pupils, but was eventually accused of corrupting the youths' minds in Athens and would be sentenced to death. As he died, he used the moment as a final lesson for his students and followers to show them they must always be calm in the face of adversity and keep moving forward. To die is for the soul to be free.

The Socratic Method

Due to his special way of drawing conversation and evaluating one's beliefs, Socrates was able to form something known as the Socratic method. It's still used today and is a form of cooperative dialogue between individuals, based on asking and answering questions to stimulate critical thinking and draw out ideas and underlying presuppositions. Socrates would use this method in order to challenge politicians about their beliefs and would at the end often leave them looking stupid and lost for words. It's more than likely that this played a part in them sentencing him to death.

We Know Nothing

Socrates taught that the only true knowledge was the acknowledgement of the fact we don't know anything. Although it may seem quite harsh when taken at face value, his intention here was that it's rare that people are aware that we can't be sure of anything, even existence (a philosophical problem which was later answered by Descartes). All aspects of reality must be questioned.

Concept of the Self

Socrates believed that soul and self simply means a thinking willing subject. Ultimate wisdom comes from knowing oneself. This is the essence of what human beings are and should be. When we take the time to repeatedly look inward at ourselves asking what we want, who we are and all the other important questions, we will eventually get to an answer and find ourselves. Socrates believed a good life can be reached by training our souls in the acquisition of knowledge, wisdom and virtue.

～

5 Facts About Socrates

1. Socrates believed that he knew nothing.

2. Socrates served in the military during the Peloponnesian war.
3. Socrates, although married, was thought of at the time to be bisexual.
4. The poison given to Socrates was known as Hemlock.
5. He learned masonry from his father at a young age.

83 SOCRATES QUOTES

"EMPLOY YOUR TIME IN IMPROVING YOURSELF BY OTHER MEN'S WRITINGS SO THAT YOU SHALL COME EASILY BY WHAT OTHERS HAVE LABOURED HARD FOR."

"WELL I AM CERTAINLY WISER THAN THIS MAN. IT IS ONLY TOO LIKELY THAT NEITHER OF US HAS ANY KNOWLEDGE TO BOAST OF; BUT HE THINKS THAT HE KNOWS SOMETHING WHICH HE DOES NOT KNOW, WHEREAS I AM QUITE CONSCIOUS OF MY IGNORANCE. AT ANY RATE IT SEEMS THAT I AM WISER THAN HE IS TO THIS SMALL EXTENT, THAT I DO NOT THINK THAT I KNOW WHAT I DO NOT KNOW."

"THE BEGINNING OF WISDOM IS A DEFINITION OF TERMS."

"WHAT A LOT OF THINGS THERE ARE THAT A MAN CAN DO WITHOUT."

"I CANNOT TEACH ANYBODY ANYTHING. I CAN ONLY MAKE THEM THINK."

"SLANDERERS DO NOT HURT ME BECAUSE THEY DO NOT HIT ME."

"I WAS AFRAID THAT BY OBSERVING OBJECTS WITH MY EYES AND TRYING TO COMPREHEND THEM WITH EACH OF MY OTHER SENSES I MIGHT BLIND MY SOUL ALTOGETHER."

"HE WHO IS NOT CONTENT WITH WHAT HE HAS, WOULD NOT BE CONTENT WITH WHAT HE WOULD LIKE TO HAVE."

"IF A MAN IS PROUD OF HIS WEALTH, HE SHOULD NOT BE PRAISED UNTIL IT IS KNOWN HOW HE EMPLOYS IT."

"WHERE THERE IS REVERENCE THERE IS FEAR, BUT THERE IS NOT REVERENCE EVERYWHERE THAT THERE IS FEAR, BECAUSE FEAR PRESUMABLY HAS A WIDER EXTENSION THAN REVERENCE."

"THEY ARE NOT ONLY IDLE WHO DO NOTHING, BUT THEY ARE IDLE ALSO WHO MIGHT BE BETTER EMPLOYED."

"OUR PRAYERS SHOULD BE FOR BLESSINGS IN GENERAL, FOR GOD KNOWS BEST WHAT IS GOOD FOR US."

"I ONLY WISH THAT ORDINARY PEOPLE HAD AN UNLIMITED CAPACITY FOR DOING HARM; THEN THEY MIGHT HAVE AN UNLIMITED POWER FOR DOING GOOD."

"I WAS REALLY TOO HONEST A MAN TO BE A POLITICIAN AND LIVE."

"ORDINARY PEOPLE SEEM NOT TO REALISE THAT THOSE WHO REALLY APPLY THEMSELVES IN THE RIGHT WAY TO PHILOSOPHY ARE DIRECTLY AND OF THEIR OWN ACCORD PREPARING THEMSELVES FOR DYING AND DEATH."

"SEE ONE PROMONTORY, ONE MOUNTAIN, ONE SEA, ONE RIVER AND SEE ALL."

"A SYSTEM OF MORALITY WHICH IS BASED ON RELATIVE EMOTIONAL VALUES IS A MERE ILLUSION, A THOROUGHLY VULGAR CONCEPTION WHICH HAS NOTHING SOUND IN IT AND NOTHING TRUE."

"BY ALL MEANS MARRY. IF YOU GET A GOOD WIFE YOU WILL BECOME HAPPY, AND IF YOU GET A BAD ONE YOU WILL BECOME A PHILOSOPHER."

"WHEN DESIRE, HAVING REJECTED REASON AND OVERPOWERED JUDGMENT WHICH LEADS TO RIGHT, IS SET IN THE DIRECTION OF THE PLEASURE WHICH BEAUTY CAN INSPIRE, AND WHEN AGAIN UNDER THE INFLUENCE OF ITS KINDRED DESIRES IT IS MOVED WITH VIOLENT MOTION TOWARDS THE BEAUTY OF CORPOREAL FORMS, IT ACQUIRES A SURNAME FROM THIS VERY VIOLENT MOTION, AND IS CALLED LOVE."

"I PRAY TO THE GODS, THAT I MAY BE BEAUTIFUL WITHIN."

"NATURE HAS GIVEN US TWO EARS, TWO EYES, AND BUT ONE TONGUE TO THE END THAT WE SHOULD HEAR AND SEE MORE THAN WE SPEAK."

"IN CHILDHOOD BE MODEST, IN YOUTH TEMPERATE, IN ADULTHOOD JUST, AND IN OLD AGE PRUDENT."

"WE ARE IN FACT CONVINCED THAT IF WE ARE EVER TO HAVE PURE KNOWLEDGE OF ANYTHING, WE MUST GET RID OF THE BODY AND CONTEMPLATE THINGS BY THEMSELVES WITH THE SOUL BY ITSELF. IT SEEMS, TO JUDGE FROM THE ARGUMENT, THAT THE WISDOM WHICH WE DESIRE AND UPON WHICH WE PROFESS TO HAVE SET OUR HEARTS WILL BE ATTAINABLE ONLY WHEN WE ARE DEAD AND NOT IN OUR LIFETIME."

"NOTHING IS TO BE PREFERRED BEFORE JUSTICE."

"LET HIM THAT WOULD MOVE THE WORLD, FIRST MOVE HIMSELF."

"THE COMIC AND THE TRAGIC LIE INSEPARABLY CLOSE, LIKE LIGHT AND SHADOW."

"I AM NOT AN ATHENIAN, NOR A GREEK, BUT A CITIZEN OF THE WORLD."

"WARS AND REVOLUTIONS AND BATTLES ARE DUE SIMPLY AND SOLELY TO THE BODY AND ITS DESIRES. ALL WARS ARE UNDERTAKEN FOR THE ACQUISITION OF WEALTH; AND THE REASON WHY WE HAVE TO ACQUIRE WEALTH IS THE BODY, BECAUSE WE ARE SLAVES IN ITS SERVICE."

"NO MAN UNDERTAKES A TRADE HE HAS NOT LEARNED, EVEN THE MEANEST; YET EVERYONE THINKS HIMSELF SUFFICIENTLY QUALIFIED FOR THE HARDEST OF ALL TRADES, THAT OF GOVERNMENT."

"CALL NO MAN UNHAPPY UNTIL HE IS MARRIED."

"HAPPINESS IS UNREPENTANT PLEASURE."

"THE ONLY GOOD IS KNOWLEDGE AND THE ONLY EVIL IS IGNORANCE."

"THE NEAREST WAY TO GLORY IS TO STRIVE TO BE WHAT YOU WISH TO BE THOUGHT TO BE."

"BE SLOW TO FALL INTO FRIENDSHIP; BUT WHEN THOU ART IN, CONTINUE FIRM AND CONSTANT."

"WORTHLESS PEOPLE LOVE ONLY TO EAT AND DRINK; PEOPLE OF WORTH EAT AND DRINK ONLY TO LIVE."

"ONCE MADE EQUAL TO MAN, WOMAN BECOMES HIS SUPERIOR."

"FAME IS THE PERFUME OF HEROIC DEEDS."

"THE ENVIOUS PERSON GROWS LEAN WITH THE FATNESS OF THEIR NEIGHBOUR."

"AN EDUCATION OBTAINED WITH MONEY IS WORSE THAN NO EDUCATION AT ALL."

"WHOM DO I CALL EDUCATED? FIRST, THOSE WHO MANAGE WELL THE CIRCUMSTANCES THEY ENCOUNTER DAY BY DAY. NEXT, THOSE WHO ARE DECENT AND HONOURABLE IN THEIR INTERCOURSE WITH ALL MEN, BEARING EASILY AND GOOD NATUREDLY WHAT IS OFFENSIVE IN OTHERS AND BEING AS AGREEABLE AND REASONABLE TO THEIR ASSOCIATES AS IS HUMANLY POSSIBLE TO BE... THOSE WHO HOLD THEIR PLEASURES ALWAYS UNDER CONTROL AND ARE NOT ULTIMATELY OVERCOME BY THEIR MISFORTUNES... THOSE WHO ARE NOT SPOILED BY THEIR SUCCESSES, WHO DO NOT DESERT THEIR TRUE SELVES BUT HOLD THEIR GROUND STEADFASTLY AS WISE AND SOBER MINDED MEN."

"FALSE WORDS ARE NOT ONLY EVIL IN THEMSELVES, BUT THEY INFECT THE SOUL WITH EVIL."

"THE FEWER OUR WANTS THE MORE WE RESEMBLE THE GODS."

"LIFE CONTAINS BUT TWO TRAGEDIES. ONE IS NOT TO GET YOUR HEART'S DESIRE; THE OTHER IS TO GET IT."

"WHENEVER, THEREFORE, PEOPLE ARE DECEIVED AND FORM OPINIONS WIDE OF THE TRUTH, IT IS CLEAR THAT THE ERROR HAS SLID INTO THEIR MINDS THROUGH THE MEDIUM OF CERTAIN RESEMBLANCES TO THAT TRUTH."

"IF I TELL YOU THAT I WOULD BE DISOBEYING THE GOD AND ON THAT ACCOUNT IT IS IMPOSSIBLE FOR ME TO KEEP QUIET, YOU WON'T BE PERSUADED BY ME, TAKING IT THAT I AM IONISING. AND IF I TELL YOU THAT IT IS THE GREATEST GOOD FOR A HUMAN BEING TO HAVE DISCUSSIONS EVERY DAY ABOUT VIRTUE AND THE OTHER THINGS YOU HEAR ME TALKING ABOUT, EXAMINING MYSELF AND OTHERS, AND THAT THE UNEXAMINED LIFE IS NOT LIVEABLE FOR A HUMAN BEING, YOU WILL BE EVEN LESS PERSUADED."

"THE HOUR OF DEPARTURE HAS ARRIVED AND WE GO OUR WAYS; I TO DIE, AND YOU TO LIVE. WHICH IS BETTER? ONLY GOD KNOWS."

"TO FEAR DEATH, MY FRIENDS, IS ONLY TO THINK OURSELVES WISE, WITHOUT BEING WISE: FOR IT IS TO THINK THAT WE KNOW WHAT WE DO NOT KNOW. FOR ANYTHING THAT MEN CAN TELL, DEATH MAY BE THE GREATEST GOOD THAT CAN HAPPEN TO THEM: BUT THEY FEAR IT AS IF THEY KNEW QUITE WELL THAT IT WAS THE GREATEST OF EVILS. AND WHAT IS THIS BUT THAT SHAMEFUL IGNORANCE OF THINKING THAT WE KNOW WHAT WE DO NOT KNOW?"

"THINK NOT THOSE FAITHFUL WHO PRAISE ALL THY WORDS AND ACTIONS, BUT THOSE WHO KINDLY REPROVE THY FAULTS."

"GIVE ME BEAUTY IN THE INWARD SOUL; MAY THE OUTWARD AND THE INWARD MAN BE AT ONE."

"HE IS RICH WHO IS CONTENT WITH THE LEAST; FOR CONTENTMENT IS THE WEALTH OF NATURE."

"REMEMBER, NO HUMAN CONDITION IS EVER PERMANENT. THEN YOU WILL NOT BE OVERJOYED IN GOOD FORTUNE NOR TOO SCORNFUL IN MISFORTUNE."

"BEAUTY IS A SHORT-LIVED TYRANNY."

"BE KIND, FOR EVERYONE YOU MEET IS FIGHTING A HARD BATTLE."

"EVERY ACTION HAS ITS PLEASURES AND ITS PRICE."

"REMEMBER WHAT IS UNBECOMING TO DO IS ALSO UNBECOMING TO SPEAK OF."

"BE AS YOU WISH TO SEEM."

"DO NOT DO TO OTHERS WHAT ANGERS YOU
IF DONE TO YOU BY OTHERS."

"ARE YOU NOT ASHAMED OF HEAPING UP
THE GREATEST AMOUNT OF MONEY AND
HONOUR AND REPUTATION, AND CARING SO
LITTLE ABOUT WISDOM AND TRUTH AND
THE GREATEST IMPROVEMENT OF THE
SOUL?"

"REMEMBER THAT THERE IS NOTHING
STABLE IN HUMAN AFFAIRS; THEREFORE
AVOID UNDUE ELATION IN PROSPERITY, OR
UNDUE DEPRESSION IN ADVERSITY."

"WE CANNOT LIVE BETTER THAN IN
SEEKING TO BECOME BETTER."

"SMART PEOPLE LEARN FROM EVERYTHING
AND EVERYONE, AVERAGE PEOPLE FROM
THEIR EXPERIENCES, STUPID PEOPLE
ALREADY HAVE ALL THE ANSWERS."

"THE HIGHEST REALMS OF THOUGHT ARE
IMPOSSIBLE TO REACH WITHOUT FIRST
ATTAINING AN UNDERSTANDING OF
COMPASSION."

"THE EASIEST AND NOBLEST WAY IS NOT TO
BE CRUSHING OTHERS, BUT TO BE
IMPROVING YOURSELVES."

"WHEN YOU WANT WISDOM AND INSIGHT AS
BADLY AS YOU WANT TO BREATHE, IT IS
THEN YOU SHALL HAVE IT."

"THROUGH YOUR RAGS I SEE YOUR VANITY."

"EDUCATION IS THE KINDLING OF A FLAME,
NOT THE FILLING OF A VESSEL."

"THE SHORTEST AND SUREST WAY TO LIVE WITH HONOUR IN THE WORLD, IS TO BE IN REALITY WHAT WE WOULD APPEAR TO BE; AND IF WE OBSERVE, WE SHALL FIND THAT ALL HUMAN VIRTUES INCREASE AND STRENGTHEN THEMSELVES BY THE PRACTICE OF THEM."

"NO MAN HAS THE RIGHT TO BE AN AMATEUR IN THE MATTER OF PHYSICAL TRAINING. IT IS A SHAME FOR A MAN TO GROW OLD WITHOUT SEEING THE BEAUTY AND STRENGTH OF WHICH HIS BODY IS CAPABLE."

"I KNOW NOTHING EXCEPT THE FACT OF MY IGNORANCE."

"IF YOU DON'T GET WHAT YOU WANT, YOU SUFFER; IF YOU GET WHAT YOU DON'T WANT, YOU SUFFER; EVEN WHEN YOU GET EXACTLY WHAT YOU WANT, YOU STILL SUFFER BECAUSE YOU CAN'T HOLD ON TO IT FOREVER. YOUR MIND IS YOUR PREDICAMENT. IT WANTS TO BE FREE OF CHANGE. FREE OF PAIN, FREE OF THE OBLIGATIONS OF LIFE AND DEATH. BUT CHANGE IS LAW AND NO AMOUNT OF PRETENDING WILL ALTER THAT REALITY."

"THERE ARE TWO KINDS OF DISEASE OF THE SOUL, VICE AND IGNORANCE."

"SOMETIMES YOU PUT WALLS UP NOT TO KEEP PEOPLE OUT, BUT TO SEE WHO CARES ENOUGH TO BREAK THEM DOWN."

"STRONG MINDS DISCUSS IDEAS, AVERAGE MINDS DISCUSS EVENTS, WEAK MINDS DISCUSS PEOPLE."

"THE SECRET OF HAPPINESS, YOU SEE, IS NOT FOUND IN SEEKING MORE, BUT IN DEVELOPING THE CAPACITY TO ENJOY LESS."

"FALLING DOWN IS NOT A FAILURE. FAILURE COMES WHEN YOU STAY WHERE YOU HAVE FALLEN."

"PREFER KNOWLEDGE TO WEALTH, FOR THE ONE IS TRANSITORY, THE OTHER PERPETUAL."

"GET NOT YOUR FRIENDS BY COMPLIMENTS, BUT BY GIVING THEM SENSIBLE TOKENS OF YOUR LOVE."

"IF YOU WANT TO BE A GOOD SADDLER, SADDLE THE WORST HORSE; FOR IF YOU CAN TAME ONE, YOU CAN TAME ALL."

"ONE SHOULD NEVER DO WRONG IN RETURN, NOR MISTREAT ANY MAN, NO MATTER HOW ONE HAS BEEN MISTREATED BY HIM."

"THE GREATEST WAY TO LIVE WITH HONOUR IN THIS WORLD IS TO BE WHAT WE PRETEND TO BE."

"IF ALL OUR MISFORTUNES WERE LAID IN ONE COMMON HEAP WHENCE EVERYONE MUST TAKE AN EQUAL PORTION, MOST PEOPLE WOULD BE CONTENT TO TAKE THEIR OWN AND DEPART."

"THE GREATEST BLESSING GRANTED TO MANKIND COMES BY WAY OF MADNESS, WHICH IS A DIVINE GIFT."

"THE YEARS WRINKLE OUR SKIN, BUT LACK OF ENTHUSIASM WRINKLES OUR SOUL."

ARISTOTLE

*A*ristotle was born in Macedonia, circa 384 BC. Aristotle was born into a relatively wealthy family, with his father being the doctor of the city. He was a direct student of Plato and just like his teacher, he would go on to become one of the most influential philosophers of his time. So much so, that he had nicknames like 'The Master' and 'The Philosopher'. Aristotle joined Plato when he was just 17. He famously taught Alexander the Great, one of the most famous conquerors of all time. Aristotle also founded a secondary school of his own, which was called the Peripatetic school.

Aristotle was a very curious man and always seemed to have a fascination with the way things work. He loved to ask the questions of how and why. How do things operate? Why is there order? How does the sunrise and fall seemingly every day without signs of waver? What makes a society function cohesively together? Aristotle's views and outlook on the world would be passed on to even as far as medieval scholars and their works.

In Aristotle's time, he managed to accumulate an impressive portfolio, with his most famous bodies of work including *Nicomachean Ethics, Metaphysics* and *The Organon*.

Virtues

Aristotle strongly believed that there are certain virtues that make a man good.

Courage, temperance, magnificence, magnanimity, pride, patience, truthfulness, wittiness, friendliness and modesty are the virtues seen as the 'golden mean'.

Aristotle taught that we should take the time to evaluate and analyse these threats; in doing so, we can begin to understand how we can incorporate these characteristics into ourselves.

Aristotle also strongly believed that a good conversation is an integral part of a good life. With each virtue,

Aristotle believed that on either end there are two opposing extremes of the characteristics. To give you an example of what he meant, on one extreme in the virtue of wittiness, there is boredom, where someone lacks communication skills and simply isn't a joy to be around. On the other extreme, there is a buffoon who will do anything at the cost of a laugh or to get the attention of others. This can come even at the expense of damaged integrity.

Aristotle understood that although the virtues we have can't be instantly changed with the flick of a finger, he appreciated the fact that virtues can be trained and formed as a habit. With good repeated practice, good virtues can become habitual acts.

The Purpose of Tragedy

Aristotle was fascinated by the concept of tragedy and why it's so important in our lives and culture. Aristotle believed that tragedy teaches us something very important, it reminds us that very bad things can happen to very good people at any point in life. You could have the perfect student, partner, soldier who lived a good moral life but with one simple mistake, their lives could alter and change for the worse, forever. Therefore, we must show great compassion for people who have done wrong in their past and now find themselves in a struggling situation. We should show pity for our neighbours and people in our society who have been cast aside for mistakes they committed.

The Importance of Friends

Aristotle divided friends into three different types.

Social friends: these are the people one might meet for leisurely activities like drinking. Strategic friends: these are people who can be seen as acquaintances, for example, some political figures.

Lastly, we have real friends. Aristotle believed that to be a real friend with someone who cares for you just as much as you care for yourself. They feel your pain, happiness, joy and sorrow. You are attached in a special way. You are able to freely and comfortably share your most intimate parts with each other. Your minds become one. You grow and progress with each other and you challenge each others' beliefs and behaviours. Aristotle believed that having a true friend in this world is one of life's greatest gifts.

5 Facts About Aristotle

1. Aristotle did not believe in Plato's theory of the forms but rather believed in empiricism.
2. Aristotle loved to walk and converse; he would often have his students go with him for a walk around the lyceum.
3. To honour his son, he named one of his books *'Nicomachean Ethics'* after his son, Nicomachus.
4. Aristotle hated public debates and much preferred a close encounter with people.
5. After the death of his father Nicomachus, Proxenus – husband of Aristotle's sister Arimneste, became the guardian of young Aristotle.

109 ARISTOTLE QUOTES

"HAPPINESS IS ACTIVITY."

"THE DIFFERENCE BETWEEN A LEARNED MAN AND AN IGNORANT ONE IS THE SAME AS THAT BETWEEN A LIVING MAN AND A CORPSE."

"POETRY DEMANDS A MAN WITH A SPECIAL GIFT FOR IT, OR ELSE ONE WITH A TOUCH OF MADNESS IN HIM."

"ALL HUMAN ACTIONS HAVE ONE OR MORE OF THESE SEVEN CAUSES: CHANCE, NATURE, COMPULSIONS, HABIT, REASON, PASSION, DESIRE."

"A FRIEND TO ALL IS A FRIEND TO NONE."

"CHARACTER MAY ALMOST BE CALLED THE MOST EFFECTIVE MEANS OF PERSUASION."

"IT IS WELL TO BE UP BEFORE DAYBREAK, FOR SUCH HABITS CONTRIBUTE TO HEALTH, WEALTH, AND WISDOM."

"THROUGH DISCIPLINE COMES FREEDOM."

"TO BE CONSCIOUS THAT WE ARE PERCEIVING OR THINKING IS TO BE CONSCIOUS OF OUR OWN EXISTENCE."

"MEN CREATE GODS AFTER THEIR OWN IMAGE, NOT ONLY WITH REGARD TO THEIR FORM BUT WITH REGARD TO THEIR MODE OF LIFE."

"ANYBODY CAN BECOME ANGRY – THAT IS EASY, BUT TO BE ANGRY WITH THE RIGHT PERSON AND TO THE RIGHT DEGREE AND AT THE RIGHT TIME AND FOR THE RIGHT PURPOSE, AND IN THE RIGHT WAY – THAT IS NOT WITHIN EVERYBODY'S POWER AND IS NOT EASY."

"THE HAPPY LIFE IS REGARDED AS A LIFE IN CONFORMITY WITH VIRTUE. IT IS A LIFE WHICH INVOLVES EFFORT AND IS NOT SPENT IN AMUSEMENT."

"EXCELLENCE IS AN ART WON BY TRAINING AND HABITUATION. WE DO NOT ACT RIGHTLY BECAUSE WE HAVE VIRTUE OR EXCELLENCE, BUT WE RATHER HAVE THOSE BECAUSE WE HAVE ACTED RIGHTLY. WE ARE WHAT WE REPEATEDLY DO. EXCELLENCE, THEN, IS NOT AN ACT BUT A HABIT."

"ALL HUMAN BEINGS, BY NATURE, DESIRE TO KNOW."

"COURAGE IS THE FIRST OF HUMAN QUALITIES BECAUSE IT IS THE QUALITY WHICH GUARANTEES THE OTHERS."

"A LIKELY IMPOSSIBILITY IS ALWAYS PREFERABLE TO AN UNCONVINCING POSSIBILITY."

"CRITICISM IS SOMETHING WE CAN AVOID EASILY BY SAYING NOTHING, DOING NOTHING, AND BEING NOTHING."

"DEMOCRACY IS WHEN THE INDIGENT, AND NOT THE MEN OF PROPERTY, ARE THE RULERS."

"THE ANTIDOTE FOR FIFTY ENEMIES IS ONE FRIEND."

"DIGNITY DOES NOT CONSIST IN POSSESSING HONOURS, BUT IN DESERVING THEM."

"EACH MAN JUDGES WELL THE THINGS HE KNOWS."

"TO LOVE SOMEONE IS TO IDENTIFY WITH THEM."

"WE CANNOT LEARN WITHOUT PAIN."

"EDUCATING THE MIND WITHOUT EDUCATING THE HEART IS NO EDUCATION AT ALL."

"THE LEAST INITIAL DEVIATION FROM THE TRUTH IS MULTIPLIED LATER A THOUSAND FOLD."

"THE MOST PERFECT POLITICAL COMMUNITY IS ONE IN WHICH THE MIDDLE CLASS IS IN CONTROL, AND OUTNUMBERS BOTH OF THE OTHER CLASSES."

"EQUALITY CONSISTS IN THE SAME TREATMENT OF SIMILAR PERSONS."

"EXCELLENCE IS NEVER AN ACCIDENT. IT IS ALWAYS THE RESULT OF HIGH INTENTION, SINCERE EFFORT, AND INTELLIGENT EXECUTION; IT REPRESENTS THE WISE CHOICE OF MANY ALTERNATIVES – CHOICE, NOT CHANCE, DETERMINES YOUR DESTINY."

"THE ROOTS OF EDUCATION ARE BITTER, BUT THE FRUIT IS SWEET."

"THE SECRET TO HUMOUR IS SURPRISE."

"FEAR IS PAIN ARISING FROM THE
ANTICIPATION OF EVIL."

"COMEDY AIMS AT REPRESENTING MEN AS
WORSE, TRAGEDY AS BETTER THAN IN
ACTUAL LIFE."

"FRIENDS HOLD A MIRROR UP TO EACH
OTHER; THROUGH THAT MIRROR THEY CAN
SEE EACH OTHER IN WAYS THAT WOULD
NOT OTHERWISE BE ACCESSIBLE TO THEM,
AND IT IS THIS MIRRORING THAT HELPS
THEM IMPROVE THEMSELVES AS PERSONS."

"IT IS EASY TO PERFORM A GOOD ACTION,
BUT NOT EASY TO ACQUIRE A SETTLED
HABIT OF PERFORMING SUCH ACTIONS."

"GOOD HABITS FORMED AT YOUTH MAKE ALL
THE DIFFERENCE."

"HAPPINESS DEPENDS UPON OURSELVES."

"AT HIS BEST, MAN IS THE NOBLEST OF ALL ANIMALS; SEPARATED FROM LAW AND JUSTICE HE IS THE WORST."

"HAPPINESS IS AN EXPRESSION OF THE SOUL IN CONSIDERED ACTIONS."

"THE ONE EXCLUSIVE SIGN OF THOROUGH KNOWLEDGE IS THE POWER OF TEACHING."

"THE PROOF THAT YOU KNOW SOMETHING IS THAT YOU ARE ABLE TO TEACH IT."

"HE WHO HAS NEVER LEARNED TO OBEY CANNOT BE A GOOD COMMANDER."

"THE SOCIETY THAT LOSES ITS GRIP ON THE PAST IS IN DANGER, FOR IT PRODUCES MEN WHO KNOW NOTHING BUT THE PRESENT, AND WHO ARE NOT AWARE THAT LIFE HAD BEEN, AND COULD BE, DIFFERENT FROM WHAT IT IS."

"EVEN WHEN LAWS HAVE BEEN WRITTEN DOWN, THEY OUGHT NOT ALWAYS TO REMAIN UNALTERED."

"THE ULTIMATE VALUE OF LIFE DEPENDS UPON AWARENESS AND THE POWER OF CONTEMPLATION RATHER THAN UPON MERE SURVIVAL."

"HE WHO IS TO BE A GOOD RULER MUST HAVE FIRST BEEN RULED."

"EVERY RASCAL IS NOT A THIEF, BUT EVERY THIEF IS A RASCAL."

"HOPE IS A WAKING DREAM."

"I COUNT HIM BRAVER WHO OVERCOMES HIS DESIRES THAN HIM WHO CONQUERS HIS ENEMIES; FOR THE HARDEST VICTORY IS OVER SELF."

"I HAVE GAINED THIS BY PHILOSOPHY THAT I DO WITHOUT BEING COMMANDED WHAT OTHERS DO ONLY FROM FEAR OF THE LAW."

"IN ALL THINGS OF NATURE THERE IS SOMETHING OF THE MARVELLOUS."

"WHY IS IT THAT ALL THOSE WHO HAVE BECOME EMINENT IN PHILOSOPHY, POLITICS, POETRY, OR THE ARTS ARE CLEARLY OF AN ATRABILIOUS TEMPERAMENT AND SOME OF THEM TO SUCH AN EXTENT AS TO BE AFFECTED BY DISEASES CAUSED BY BLACK BILE?"

"IT IS DURING OUR DARKEST MOMENTS THAT WE MUST FOCUS TO SEE THE LIGHT."

"LIARS WHEN THEY SPEAK THE TRUTH ARE NOT BELIEVED."

"LOVE IS COMPOSED OF SINGLE SOUL INHABITING TWO BODIES."

"MAN IS A GOAL SEEKING ANIMAL. HIS LIFE ONLY HAS MEANING IF HE IS REACHING OUT AND STRIVING FOR HIS GOALS."

"FRIENDSHIP IS ESSENTIALLY A PARTNERSHIP."

"WICKED MEN OBEY FROM FEAR; GOOD MEN, FROM LOVE."

"MEN ACQUIRE PARTICULAR QUALITY BY CONSTANTLY ACTING IN A PARTICULAR WAY."

"THE GODS TOO ARE FOND OF A JOKE."

"THE GREATEST THING BY FAR IS TO BE A MASTER OF METAPHOR; IT IS THE ONE THING THAT CANNOT BE LEARNED FROM OTHERS; AND IT IS ALSO A SIGN OF GENIUS, SINCE A GOOD METAPHOR IMPLIES AN INTUITIVE PERCEPTION OF THE SIMILARITY OF THE DISSIMILAR."

"MEN ARE SWAYED MORE BY FEAR THAN BY REVERENCE."

"THE EDUCATED DIFFER FROM THE UNEDUCATED AS MUCH AS THE LIVING FROM THE DEAD."

"THE ENERGY OF THE MIND IS THE ESSENCE OF LIFE."

"MISFORTUNE SHOWS THOSE WHO ARE NOT REALLY FRIENDS."

"THE LEAST INITIAL DEVIATION FROM THE TRUTH IS MULTIPLIED LATER A THOUSAND FOLD."

"MOST PEOPLE WOULD RATHER GIVE THAN GET AFFECTION."

"MY BEST FRIEND IS THE MAN WHO IN WISHING ME WELL, WISHES IT FOR MY SAKE."

"NO NOTICE IS TAKEN OF A LITTLE EVIL, BUT WHEN IT INCREASES IT STRIKES THE EYE."

"NO ONE WOULD CHOOSE A FRIENDLESS EXISTENCE ON CONDITION OF HAVING ALL THE OTHER THINGS IN THE WORLD."

"OBSTINATE PEOPLE CAN BE DIVIDED INTO THE OPINIONATED, THE IGNORANT, AND THE BOORISH."

"MAN IS BY NATURE A POLITICAL ANIMAL."

"OF ALL THE VARIETIES OF VIRTUES, LIBERALISM IS THE MOST BELOVED."

"PERFECT FRIENDSHIP IS THE FRIENDSHIP OF MEN WHO ARE GOOD, AND ALIKE IN EXCELLENCE; FOR THESE WISH WELL ALIKE TO EACH OTHER QUA GOOD, AND THEY ARE GOOD IN THEMSELVES."

"HAPPINESS IS THE SETTLING OF THE SOUL INTO ITS MOST APPROPRIATE SPOT."

"IT IS POSSIBLE TO FAIL IN MANY WAYS...
WHILE TO SUCCEED IS POSSIBLE ONLY IN
ONE WAY."

"EDUCATION IS AN ORNAMENT IN
PROSPERITY AND A REFUGE IN ADVERSITY."

"HE WHO HAS NEVER LEARNED TO OBEY
CANNOT BE A GOOD COMMANDER."

"PIETY REQUIRES US TO HONOUR TRUTH
ABOVE OUR FRIENDS."

"IT IS THE MARK OF AN EDUCATED MIND TO
BE ABLE TO ENTERTAIN A THOUGHT
WITHOUT ACCEPTING IT."

"PLEASURE IN THE JOB PUTS PERFECTION IN
THE WORK."

"THE TRUE AND THE APPROXIMATELY TRUE ARE APPREHENDED BY THE SAME FACULTY; IT MAY ALSO BE NOTED THAT MEN HAVE A SUFFICIENT NATURAL INSTINCT FOR WHAT IS TRUE, AND USUALLY DO ARRIVE AT THE TRUTH. HENCE THE MAN WHO MAKES A GOOD GUESS AT TRUTH IS LIKELY TO MAKE A GOOD GUESS AT PROBABILITIES."

"THE IDEAL MAN BEARS THE ACCIDENTS OF LIFE WITH DIGNITY AND GRACE, MAKING THE BEST OF CIRCUMSTANCES."

"WE PRAISE A MAN WHO FEELS ANGRY ON THE RIGHT GROUNDS AND AGAINST THE RIGHT PERSONS AND ALSO IN THE RIGHT MANNER AT THE RIGHT MOMENT AND FOR THE RIGHT LENGTH OF TIME."

"THE WORST FORM OF INEQUALITY IS TO TRY TO MAKE UNEQUAL THINGS EQUAL."

"POVERTY IS THE PARENT OF REVOLUTION AND CRIME."

"THERE IS NO GREAT GENIUS WITHOUT SOME TOUCH OF MADNESS."

"POETRY IS FINER AND MORE PHILOSOPHICAL THAN HISTORY; FOR POETRY EXPRESSES THE UNIVERSAL, AND HISTORY ONLY THE PARTICULAR."

"THE BEAUTY OF THE SOUL SHINES OUT WHEN A MAN BEARS WITH COMPOSURE ONE HEAVY MISCHANCE AFTER ANOTHER, NOT BECAUSE HE DOES NOT FEEL THEM, BUT BECAUSE HE IS A MAN OF HIGH AND HEROIC TEMPER."

"PROBABLE IMPOSSIBILITIES ARE TO BE PREFERRED TO IMPROBABLE POSSIBILITIES."

"QUALITY IS NOT AN ACT, IT IS A HABIT."

"THE EDUCATED DIFFER FROM THE UNEDUCATED AS MUCH AS THE LIVING FROM THE DEAD."

SIMPLY PHILOSOPHICAL QUOTES

"REPUBLICS DECLINE INTO DEMOCRACIES AND DEMOCRACIES DEGENERATE INTO DESPOTISM."

"SOMETHING IS INFINITE IF, TAKING IT QUANTITY BY QUANTITY, WE CAN ALWAYS TAKE SOMETHING OUTSIDE."

"THE ACTUALITY OF THOUGHT IS LIFE."

"WHOSOEVER IS DELIGHTED IN SOLITUDE IS EITHER A WILD BEAST OR A GOD."

"THE AIM OF THE WISE IS NOT TO SECURE PLEASURE, BUT TO AVOID PAIN."

"THIS IS THE REASON WHY MOTHERS ARE MORE DEVOTED TO THEIR CHILDREN THAN FATHERS: IT IS THAT THEY SUFFER MORE IN GIVING THEM BIRTH AND ARE MORE CERTAIN THAT THEY ARE THEIR OWN."

"THOSE THAT KNOW, DO. THOSE THAT UNDERSTAND, TEACH."

"WE LIVE IN DEEDS, NOT YEARS; IN THOUGHTS, NOT BREATHS; IN FEELINGS, NOT IN FIGURES ON A DIAL. WE SHOULD COUNT TIME BY HEART THROBS. HE MOST LIVES WHO THINKS MOST, FEELS THE NOBLEST, ACTS THE BEST."

"TO WRITE WELL, EXPRESS YOURSELF LIKE COMMON PEOPLE, BUT THINK LIKE A WISE MAN. OR, THINK AS WISE MEN DO, BUT SPEAK AS THE COMMON PEOPLE DO."

"WE MUST BE NEITHER COWARDLY NOR RASH BUT COURAGEOUS."

"THOSE WHO EDUCATE CHILDREN WELL ARE MORE TO BE HONOURED THAN THEY WHO PRODUCE THEM; FOR THESE ONLY GAVE THEM LIFE, THOSE THE ART OF LIVING WELL."

"WISHING TO BE FRIENDS IS QUICK WORK, BUT FRIENDSHIP IS A SLOW-RIPENING FRUIT."

"THE AIM OF ART IS TO REPRESENT NOT THE OUTWARD APPEARANCE OF THINGS, BUT THEIR INWARD SIGNIFICANCE."

"WIT IS EDUCATED INSOLENCE."

"YOU WILL NEVER DO ANYTHING IN THE WORLD WITHOUT COURAGE. IT IS THE GREATEST QUALITY OF THE MIND NEXT TO HONOUR."

"THE ENERGY OF THE MIND IS THE ESSENCE OF LIFE."

"IT IS NOT ENOUGH TO WIN A WAR; IT IS MORE IMPORTANT TO ORGANISE THE PEACE."

FRIEDRICH NIETZCHE

*J*n 1844, Friedrich Nietzsche was born in Prussia, Germany. As a scholar, philosopher and critic of culture, he became one of the most influential modern thinkers.

From his youth, Nietzsche excelled academically - at 24 years old, he became the youngest person to be called up to a chair in classical philology at Basel. In his letter of reference, one of his university professors, Friedrich Wilhelm Ritschl, wrote that "He will simply be able to do anything he wants to do." Nietzsche would be the only student to ever contribute to one of Ritschl's journals, *Rheinisches Museum*. In the summer of 1870, Nietzsche halted his professional work to volunteer as a medical orderly during the Franco-German war. Within a month, he had contracted diphtheria and dysentery, and his health was never the same again. He returned to teaching at Basel, but as early as October the following year, his ill health forced him to take leave from teaching. In 1879, he resigned from his professional chair completely and took a pension of 3000 Swiss francs per year for six years. He would spend the next ten years half-blind, very ill and residing in boarding houses across France, Italy and Switzerland. However, these years would be of supreme productivity and he wrote many of his works during this time.

After a collapse and loss of his mental faculties in 1889, Friedrich Nietzsche sadly spent the last 11 years of his life in total mental darkness until he passed away in 1900.

Nihilism

Nietzsche is linked by scholars to nihilism, a disregard for anything that cannot be proved scientifically. However, he did not ever claim that nothing exists that cannot be proven, but rather suggested that many people use religion, particularly Judeo-Christian teachings as a means for avoiding decisive actions.

Existentialism

Nietzsche was one of the pioneers of existentialism, contributing a belief that men need to accept they are part of a material world whatever else they may believe or what may exist. Consequently, humans must believe and act as if there is nothing else beyond life because a failure to live and take risks because of non-material fear is ultimately, a failure to realise human potential.

Questioning Religion

Friedrich Nietzsche is arguably most famous for his criticism of European moral commitments, often founded in Christianity. According to Nietzsche, the Judeo-Christian tradition makes suffering tolerable and justifies it with atonement and God's intention. This led to him making the bold and paradoxical statement that "God is dead". While he didn't actually mean that atheism is necessarily true, he later explained that "the belief in the Christian God has become unbelievable" and that everything propped up by this faith i.e European morality, is "destined to collapse".

5 Facts About Friedrich Nietzsche

1. Similar to the last mentioned ideal of

Nietzsche's, he often shocked people with aphorisms - brief, pointed comments that jolted people to make them think, and if taken at face value they could seem harsh. As a result, he was often misunderstood.

2. Friedrich Nietzsche's father died when he was just 5 years old, and he consequently spent his early life in a household with 5 other females; two aunts, maternal grandmother, mother and younger sister.

3. Although he was strongly against nationalism and anti-Semitism, his name was later used by fascists to advance the very things he despised.

4. During his youth he was an avid composer, writing several compositions strongly influenced by the German Romantic Robert Schumann.

5. In the late 1860s, Nietzsche became friends with the great composer Richard Wagner. The two became very close and Nietzsche's first book, *The Birth of Tragedy from the Spirit of Music* involved Wagner's music. Eventually, Wagner's chauvinism and ani-Semitism drove the two apart.

90 FRIEDRICH NIETZSCHE QUOTES

"THERE IS ALWAYS SOME MADNESS IN LOVE. BUT THERE IS ALSO ALWAYS SOME REASON IN MADNESS."

"BEHIND EVERY REAL MAN THERE'S A CHILD HIDDEN THAT WANTS TO PLAY."

"WE LOVE LIFE, NOT BECAUSE WE ARE USED TO LIVING BUT BECAUSE WE ARE USED TO LOVING."

"ONE MUST STILL HAVE CHAOS IN ONESELF TO BE ABLE TO GIVE BIRTH TO A DANCING STAR."

"HE WHO HAS A REASON TO LIVE CAN BEAR ALMOST ANYTHING."

"THAT WHICH DOES NOT KILL US MAKES US STRONGER."

"INSANITY IN INDIVIDUALS IS SOMETHING RARE - BUT IN GROUPS, PARTIES, NATIONS AND EPOCHS, IT IS THE RULE."

"AND THOSE WHO WERE SEEN DANCING WERE THOUGHT TO BE INSANE BY THOSE WHO COULD NOT HEAR THE MUSIC."

"THOUGHTS ARE THE SHADOWS OF OUR FEELINGS - ALWAYS DARKER, EMPTIER AND SIMPLER."

"WHOEVER FIGHTS MONSTERS SHOULD SEE TO IT THAT IN THE PROCESS HE DOES NOT BECOME A MONSTER. AND IF YOU GAZE LONG ENOUGH INTO AN ABYSS, THE ABYSS WILL GAZE BACK INTO YOU."

"THE INDIVIDUAL HAS ALWAYS HAD TO STRUGGLE TO KEEP FROM BEING OVERWHELMED BY THE TRIBE. IF YOU TRY IT, YOU WILL BE LONELY OFTEN, AND SOMETIMES FRIGHTENED. BUT NO PRICE IS TOO HIGH TO PAY FOR THE PRIVILEGE OF OWNING YOURSELF."

"WHAT IS GREAT IN MAN IS THAT HE IS A BRIDGE AND NOT A GOAL."

"ALL TRULY GREAT THOUGHTS ARE CONCEIVED BY WALKING."

"TO LIVE IS TO SUFFER, TO SURVIVE IS TO FIND SOME MEANING IN THE SUFFERING."

"HE WHO WOULD LEARN TO FLY ONE DAY MUST FIRST LEARN TO STAND AND WALK AND RUN AND CLIMB AND DANCE; ONE CANNOT FLY INTO FLYING."

"IN THE CONSCIOUSNESS OF THE TRUTH HE HAS PERCEIVED, MAN NOW SEES EVERYWHERE ONLY THE AWFULNESS OR THE ABSURDITY OF EXISTENCE AND LOATHING SEIZES HIM."

"GO UP CLOSE TO YOUR FRIEND, BUT DO NOT GO OVER TO HIM! WE SHOULD ALSO RESPECT THE ENEMY IN OUR FRIEND."

"ALL THINGS ARE SUBJECT TO INTERPRETATION, WHICHEVER INTERPRETATION PREVAILS AT A GIVEN TIME IS A FUNCTION OF POWER AND NOT TRUTH."

"GOD IS DEAD. GOD REMAINS DEAD. AND WE HAVE KILLED HIM. YET HIS SHADOW STILL LOOMS. HOW SHALL WE COMFORT OURSELVES, THE MURDERERS OF ALL MURDERERS? WHAT WAS HOLIEST AND MIGHTIEST OF ALL THAT THE WORLD HAS YET OWNED HAS BLED TO DEATH UNDER OUR KNIVES; WHO WILL WIPE THIS BLOOD OFF US? WHAT WATER IS THERE FOR US TO CLEAN OURSELVES?"

"THOSE WHO CANNOT UNDERSTAND HOW TO PUT THEIR THOUGHTS ON ICE SHOULD NOT ENTER INTO THE HEAT OF DEBATE."

"IT IS NOT A LACK OF LOVE, BUT A LACK OF FRIENDSHIP THAT MAKES UNHAPPY MARRIAGES."

"WE HAVE ART IN ORDER NOT TO DIE OF THE TRUTH."

"WHEN ART DRESSES IN WORN-OUT MATERIAL IT IS MOST EASILY RECOGNISED AS ART."

"EGOISM IS THE VERY ESSENCE OF A NOBLE SOUL."

"ONE HAS TO PAY DEARLY FOR IMMORTALITY; ONE HAS TO DIE SEVERAL TIMES WHILE ONE IS STILL ALIVE."

"CONVICTIONS ARE MORE DANGEROUS FOES OF TRUTH THAN LIES."

"LOVE MATCHES, SO CALLED, HAVE ILLUSION FOR THEIR FATHER AND NEED FOR THEIR MOTHER."

"WHEN ONE HAS FINISHED BUILDING ONE'S HOUSE, ONE SUDDENLY REALISES THAT IN THE PROCESS THEY LEARNED SOMETHING THEY REALLY NEEDED TO KNOW IN THE WORST WAY - BEFORE ONE BEGAN."

"THE 'KINGDOM OF HEAVEN' IS A CONDITION OF THE HEART - NOT SOMETHING THAT COMES 'UPON THE EARTH' OR 'AFTER DEATH.'"

"A GOOD WRITER POSSESSES NOT ONLY HIS OWN SPIRIT BUT ALSO THE SPIRIT OF HIS FRIENDS."

"WHOEVER FEELS PREDESTINED TO SEE AND NOT TO BELIEVE WILL FIND ALL BELIEVERS TOO NOISY AND PUSHY: HE GUARDS AGAINST THEM."

"WHEN MARRYING, ASK YOURSELF THIS QUESTION: DO YOU BELIEVE THAT YOU WILL BE ABLE TO CONVERSE WELL WITH THIS PERSON INTO YOUR OLD AGE? EVERYTHING ELSE IN MARRIAGE IS TRANSITORY."

"NOTHING IS BEAUTIFUL, ONLY MAN: ON THIS PIECE OF NAIVETY RESTS ALL AESTHETICS, IT IS THE FIRST TRUTH OF AESTHETICS. LET US IMMEDIATELY ADD ITS SECOND: NOTHING IS UGLY BUT DEGENERATE MAN - THE DOMAIN OF AESTHETIC JUDGMENT IS THEREWITH DEFINED."

"HE WHO CANNOT GIVE ANYTHING AWAY CANNOT FEEL ANYTHING EITHER."

"LET US BEWARE OF SAYING THAT DEATH IS THE OPPOSITE OF LIFE. THE LIVING BEING IS ONLY A SPECIES OF THE DEAD, AND A VERY RARE SPECIES."

"THE TRUE MAN WANTS TWO THINGS: DANGER AND PLAY. FOR THAT REASON HE WANTS WOMAN, THE MOST DANGEROUS PLAYTHING."

"THE SUREST WAY TO CORRUPT A YOUTH IS TO INSTRUCT HIM TO HOLD IN HIGHER ESTEEM THOSE WHO THINK ALIKE THAN THOSE WHO THINK DIFFERENTLY."

"AN ARTIST HAS NO HOME IN EUROPE EXCEPT IN PARIS."

"AND WE SHOULD CONSIDER EVERY DAY LOST ON WHICH WE HAVE NOT DANCED AT LEAST ONCE. AND WE SHOULD CALL EVERY TRUTH FALSE WHICH WAS NOT ACCOMPANIED BY AT LEAST ONE LAUGH."

"AT TIMES ONE REMAINS FAITHFUL TO A CAUSE ONLY BECAUSE ITS OPPONENTS DO NOT CEASE TO BE INSIPID."

"THE WORD 'CHRISTIANITY' IS ALREADY A MISUNDERSTANDING - IN REALITY THERE HAS BEEN ONLY ONE CHRISTIAN, AND HE DIED ON THE CROSS."

"THE FUTURE INFLUENCES THE PRESENT
JUST AS MUCH AS THE PAST."

"WHOEVER DOES NOT HAVE A GOOD FATHER
SHOULD PROCURE ONE."

"THE IRRATIONALITY OF A THING IS NO
ARGUMENT AGAINST ITS EXISTENCE,
RATHER A CONDITION OF IT."

"TODAY I LOVE MYSELF AS I LOVE MY GOD:
WHO COULD CHARGE ME WITH A SIN
TODAY? I KNOW ONLY SINS AGAINST MY
GOD; BUT WHO KNOWS MY GOD?"

"THE WORLD ITSELF IS THE WILL TO POWER
- AND NOTHING ELSE! AND YOU YOURSELF
ARE THE WILL TO POWER - AND NOTHING
ELSE!"

"HE THAT HUMBLETH HIMSELF WISHES TO
BE EXALTED."

"THE MOST COMMON LIE IS THAT WHICH ONE LIES TO HIMSELF; LYING TO OTHERS IS RELATIVELY AN EXCEPTION."

"THE DEMAND TO BE LOVED IS THE GREATEST OF ALL ARROGANT PRESUMPTIONS."

"NOT NECESSITY, NOT DESIRE - NO, THE LOVE OF POWER IS THE DEMON OF MEN. LET THEM HAVE EVERYTHING - HEALTH, FOOD, A PLACE TO LIVE, ENTERTAINMENT - THEY ARE AND REMAIN UNHAPPY AND LOW-SPIRITED: FOR THE DEMON WAITS AND WAITS AND WILL BE SATISFIED."

"IF THERE IS SOMETHING TO PARDON IN EVERYTHING, THERE IS ALSO SOMETHING TO CONDEMN."

"IT IS IMPOSSIBLE TO SUFFER WITHOUT MAKING SOMEONE PAY FOR IT; EVERY COMPLAINT ALREADY CONTAINS REVENGE."

"THERE ARE HORRIBLE PEOPLE WHO, INSTEAD OF SOLVING A PROBLEM, TANGLE IT UP AND MAKE IT HARDER TO SOLVE FOR ANYONE WHO WANTS TO DEAL WITH IT. WHOEVER DOES NOT KNOW HOW TO HIT THE NAIL ON THE HEAD SHOULD BE ASKED NOT TO HIT IT AT ALL."

"WHATEVER IS DONE FOR LOVE ALWAYS OCCURS BEYOND GOOD AND EVIL."

"ADMIRATION FOR A QUALITY OR AN ART CAN BE SO STRONG THAT IT DETERS US FROM STRIVING TO POSSESS IT."

"THE ESSENCE OF ALL BEAUTIFUL ART, ALL GREAT ART, IS GRATITUDE."

"THE BEST WEAPON AGAINST AN ENEMY IS ANOTHER ENEMY."

"I CANNOT BELIEVE IN A GOD WHO WANTS TO BE PRAISED ALL THE TIME."

"TO FORGET ONE'S PURPOSE IS THE COMMONEST FORM OF STUPIDITY."

"THERE IS NOT ENOUGH LOVE AND GOODNESS IN THE WORLD TO PERMIT GIVING ANY OF IT AWAY TO IMAGINARY BEINGS."

"THERE IS MORE WISDOM IN YOUR BODY THAN IN YOUR DEEPEST PHILOSOPHY."

"WHAT CAN EVERYONE DO? PRAISE AND BLAME. THIS IS HUMAN VIRTUE, THIS IS HUMAN MADNESS."

"THE BEST AUTHOR WILL BE THE ONE WHO IS ASHAMED TO BECOME A WRITER."

"MYSTICAL EXPLANATIONS ARE THOUGHT TO BE DEEP; THE TRUTH IS THAT THEY ARE NOT EVEN SHALLOW."

"THERE ARE VARIOUS EYES. EVEN THE SPHINX HAS EYES: AND AS A RESULT THERE ARE VARIOUS TRUTHS, AND AS A RESULT THERE IS NO TRUTH."

"UNDESERVED PRAISE CAUSES MORE PANGS OF CONSCIENCE LATER THAN UNDESERVED BLAME, BUT PROBABLY ONLY FOR THIS REASON, THAT OUR POWER OF JUDGMENT ARE MORE COMPLETELY EXPOSED BY BEING OVER PRAISED THAN BY BEING UNJUSTLY UNDERESTIMATED."

"WHENEVER I CLIMB I AM FOLLOWED BY A DOG CALLED 'EGO'."

"GLANCE INTO THE WORLD JUST AS THOUGH TIME WERE GONE: AND EVERYTHING CROOKED WILL BECOME STRAIGHT TO YOU."

"ONE SHOULD DIE PROUDLY WHEN IT IS NO LONGER POSSIBLE TO LIVE PROUDLY."

"ARROGANCE ON THE PART OF THE
MERITORIOUS IS EVEN MORE OFFENSIVE TO
US THAN THE ARROGANCE OF THOSE
WITHOUT MERIT: FOR MERIT ITSELF IS
OFFENSIVE."

"NO ONE LIES SO BOLDLY AS THE MAN WHO
IS INDIGNANT."

"THE MAN OF KNOWLEDGE MUST BE ABLE
NOT ONLY TO LOVE HIS ENEMIES BUT ALSO
TO HATE HIS FRIENDS."

"TALKING MUCH ABOUT ONESELF CAN ALSO
BE A MEANS TO CONCEAL ONESELF."

"THERE ARE SLAVISH SOULS WHO CARRY
THEIR APPRECIATION FOR FAVOURS DONE
TO THEM SO FAR THAT THEY STRANGLE
THEMSELVES WITH THE ROPE OF
GRATITUDE."

"WORDS ARE BUT SYMBOLS FOR THE RELATIONS OF THINGS TO ONE ANOTHER AND TO US; NOWHERE DO THEY TOUCH UPON ABSOLUTE TRUTH."

"TO USE THE SAME WORDS IS NOT A SUFFICIENT GUARANTEE OF UNDERSTANDING; ONE MUST USE THE SAME WORDS FOR THE SAME GENUS OF INWARD EXPERIENCE; ULTIMATELY ONE MUST HAVE ONE'S EXPERIENCES IN COMMON."

"THE APHORISM IN WHICH I AM THE FIRST MASTER AMONG GERMANS, ARE THE FORMS OF 'ETERNITY'; MY AMBITION IS TO SAY IN TEN SENTENCES WHAT EVERYONE ELSE SAYS IN A BOOK - WHAT EVERYONE ELSE DOES NOT SAY IN A BOOK."

"THE DESIRE TO ANNOY NO ONE, TO HARM NO ONE, CAN EQUALLY WELL BE THE SIGN OF A JUST AS OF AN ANXIOUS DISPOSITION."

"ON THE MOUNTAINS OF TRUTH YOU CAN NEVER CLIMB IN VAIN: EITHER YOU WILL REACH A POINT HIGHER UP TODAY, OR YOU WILL BE TRAINING YOUR POWERS SO THAT YOU WILL BE ABLE TO CLIMB HIGHER TOMORROW."

"IN LARGE STATES PUBLIC EDUCATION WILL ALWAYS BE MEDIOCRE, FOR THE SAME REASON THAT IN LARGE KITCHENS THE COOKING IS USUALLY BAD."

"PEOPLE WHO HAVE GIVEN US THEIR COMPLETE CONFIDENCE BELIEVE THAT THEY HAVE A RIGHT TO OURS. THE INFERENCE IS FALSE, A GIFT CONFERS NO RIGHTS."

"SLEEPING IS NO MEAN ART: FOR ITS SAKE ONE MUST STAY AWAKE ALL DAY."

"THERE IS A ROLLICKING KINDNESS THAT LOOKS LIKE MALICE."

SIMPLY PHILOSOPHICAL QUOTES

"ANYONE WHO HAS DECLARED SOMEONE ELSE TO BE AN IDIOT, A BAD APPLE, IS ANNOYED WHEN IT TURNS OUT IN THE END THAT HE ISN'T."

"THE CHRISTIAN RESOLUTION TO FIND THE WORLD UGLY AND BAD HAS MADE THE WORLD UGLY AND BAD."

"OF ALL THAT IS WRITTEN, I LOVE ONLY WHAT A PERSON HAS WRITTEN WITH HIS OWN BLOOD."

"OUR TREASURE LIES IN THE BEEHIVE OF OUR KNOWLEDGE. WE ARE PERPETUALLY ON THE WAY THITHER, BEING BY NATURE WINGED INSECTS AND HONEY GATHERERS OF THE MIND."

"NOT WHEN TRUTH IS DIRTY, BUT WHEN IT IS SHALLOW, DOES THE ENLIGHTENED MAN DISLIKE TO WADE INTO ITS WATERS."

"REGARDING LIFE, THE WISEST MEN OF ALL AGES HAVE JUDGED ALIKE: IT IS WORTHLESS."

"YOU SAY IT IS THE GOOD CAUSE THAT HALLOWS EVEN WAR? I SAY UNTO YOU: IT IS THE GOOD WAR THAT HALLOWS ANY CAUSE."

JOHN LOCKE

*J*ohn Locke was an English philosopher and physician born in 1632, in Somerset. His works are key in the foundations of Empiricism, Liberalism and the Age of Enlightenment, ideas that all began in the 17th century and carry on today. At age 20, he started attending Christ Church, the largest college in the University of Oxford. Locke found the curriculum unsatisfying. The teachings were largely centred around the teachings of Aristotle and ignored a lot of the new ideas about nature and the origins of knowledge, a lot of which came to light from the likes of Descartes and Francis Bacon. Locke took great interest in these and became very familiar with the works of both philosophers, which would greatly influence his future work.

In 1660, the English monarchy was restored. It had been initially replaced by the Commonwealth in 1653 as the result of the civil war. This was both good and bad for John Locke; on one hand, many of his collaborators moved back to London and this led to them forming the Royal Society, which provided the stimulus for lots of scientific research. However, the new freedom resulted in lots of unruly behaviour amongst the undergraduates at Oxford, which led Locke to become very wary of quick social change. His growing up during the civil war likely fed into this apprehensiveness.

6 years later, John Locke met Lord Anthony Ashley Cooper, later first Earl of Shaftesbury. A great first impression eventually led to Lord Cooper inviting Locke to join his household in Exeter as his personal aide and physician. They were in agreement over a lot of ideas such as toleration in religion, civil liberty and the economic expansion of England, and this shaped a lot of the works that Locke would write in the future.

The two spent time exiled in France following the Earl of Shaftesbury's losing favour with Charles II in the 1670s, and later on, at the start of the next decade, the Earl was tried and acquitted for treason, so he fled to Holland in 1681, where he would die two years later. In the same year, John Locke moved to Holland. From this situation emerged John Locke's major political philo-sophical work, *Two Treatise of Government* in 1689. After a long period of ill health, he passed away in 1704.

Liberalism

John Locke is widely known as the 'Father of Liberal-ism'. This was founded on the social contract, arguing that everyone has a right to life, property, liberty - Locke famously wrote this as a man's three natural rights. The government must not violate these rights. It sought to replace absolute monarchy with representa-tive democracy and the rule of law. His definition of property as a product of someone's labour would become a foundation for both Adam Smith's capitalism and Karl Marx's socialism.

Empiricism

Empiricism emerged in Britain from Francis Bacon and was built upon by John Locke. It is the theory that knowledge predominantly comes from sensory experi-ence, rather than theory. It emphasises the importance of empirical evidence over innate ideas. To hone in on this and Locke's beliefs, he believed that all ideas come from sensation or reflection. An analogy he used for this was observing a child from birth. In *An Essay on Human Understanding*, he wrote: "I think it will be granted easily, that if a child were kept in a place where he never saw any other but black and white till he were a man, he would have no more ideas of scarlet or green, than he that from his childhood never tasted an oyster, or a pine-apple, has of those particular relishes...follow a child from its birth, and observe the alterations that time makes, and you shall find, as the mind by the senses comes more and more to be furnished with ideas, it comes to be more and more awake; thinks more, the more it has matter to think on."

Age of Enlightenment

The 'Age of Enlightenment' was a philosophical movement that held sway in Europe through the 17th and 18th centuries. Stemming from the philosophers that Locke took great interest in during his youth, both of John Locke's ideas and teachings previously mentioned are integral parts of the enlightenment movement, as the movement centred around empiricism and the sovereignty of reason, the latter being the gradual shift to reason as the standard of truth in politics and religion.

5 Facts About John Locke

1. John Locke's closest female friend was the philosopher Lady Damaris Cudworth Masham. Before she married, the two had exchanged love poems, and when Locke returned from exile, he moved into her and her husband's household.
2. Later in his life, John Locke was friends with Isaac Newton. Much of their correspondence came from chemist Robert Boyle, who was a mutual.
3. John Locke's actual name is John Locke Junior.
4. John Locke's mother died in his early years at Oxford. His father died in 1661 and his only sibling, Thomas, in 1663. Locke was left without a family by his early thirties.
5. Most of his monumental works were written when he was over the age of 60. These include: *An Essay Concerning Human Understanding* which inspects the human mind, *Two Treatise of Government* (his most important political work), *A Letter Concerning Toleration* which puts forward strong reasoning in favour of religious tolerance and *Some Thoughts Concerning Education* written in 1693, which remains one of the most important philosophical works on education in England.

81 JOHN LOCKE QUOTES

"THE ONLY FENCE AGAINST THE WORLD IS A THOROUGH KNOWLEDGE OF IT."

"I HAVE ALWAYS THOUGHT THE ACTIONS OF MEN THE BEST INTERPRETERS OF THEIR THOUGHTS."

"AS PEOPLE ARE WALKING ALL THE TIME, IN THE SAME SPOT, A PATH APPEARS."

"GOVERNMENT HAS NO OTHER END, BUT THE PRESERVATION OF PROPERTY."

"IT IS OF GREAT USE TO THE SAILOR TO KNOW THE LENGTH OF HIS LINE, THOUGH HE CANNOT WITH IT FATHOM ALL THE DEPTHS OF THE OCEAN."

"READING FURNISHES THE MIND ONLY WITH MATERIALS OF KNOWLEDGE; IT IS THINKING THAT MAKES WHAT WE READ OURS."

"EVERY MAN HAS A PROPERTY IN HIS OWN PERSON. THIS NOBODY HAS A RIGHT TO, BUT HIMSELF."

"NEW OPINIONS ARE ALWAYS SUSPECTED, AND USUALLY OPPOSED, WITHOUT ANY OTHER REASON BUT BECAUSE THEY ARE NOT ALREADY COMMON."

"THERE CANNOT BE GREATER RUDENESS THAN TO INTERRUPT ANOTHER IN THE CURRENT OF HIS DISCOURSE."

"REVERIE IS WHEN IDEAS FLOAT IN OUR MIND WITHOUT REFLECTION OR REGARD OF THE UNDERSTANDING."

"EDUCATION BEGINS THE GENTLEMAN, BUT READING, GOOD COMPANY AND REFLECTION MUST FINISH HIM."

"THE IMPROVEMENT OF UNDERSTANDING IS FOR TWO ENDS: FIRST, OUR OWN INCREASE OF KNOWLEDGE; SECONDLY, TO ENABLE US TO DELIVER THAT KNOWLEDGE TO OTHERS."

"ALL MEN ARE LIABLE TO ERROR; AND MOST MEN ARE, IN MANY POINTS, BY PASSION OR INTEREST, UNDER TEMPTATION TO IT."

"A SOUND MIND IN A SOUND BODY, IS A SHORT, BUT FULL DESCRIPTION OF A HAPPY STATE IN THIS WORLD: HE THAT HAS THESE TWO, HAS LITTLE MORE TO WISH FOR; AND HE THAT WANTS EITHER OF THEM, WILL BE LITTLE THE BETTER FOR ANYTHING ELSE."

"THERE IS FREQUENTLY MORE TO BE LEARNED FROM THE UNEXPECTED QUESTIONS OF A CHILD THAN THE DISCOURSES OF MEN."

"OUR INCOMES ARE LIKE OUR SHOES; IF TOO SMALL, THEY GALL AND PINCH US; BUT IF TOO LARGE, THEY CAUSE US TO STUMBLE AND TO TRIP."

"AN EXCELLENT MAN, LIKE PRECIOUS METAL, IS IN EVERY WAY INVARIABLE; A VILLAIN, LIKE THE BEAMS OF A BALANCE, IS ALWAYS VARYING, UPWARDS AND DOWNWARDS."

"TO PREJUDGE OTHER MEN'S NOTIONS BEFORE WE HAVE LOOKED INTO THEM IS NOT TO SHOW THEIR DARKNESS BUT TO PUT OUT OUR OWN EYES."

"THE DREAD OF EVIL IS A MUCH MORE FORCIBLE PRINCIPLE OF HUMAN ACTIONS THAN THE PROSPECT OF GOOD."

"WHERE THERE IS NO PROPERTY THERE IS NO INJUSTICE."

"TO LOVE OUR NEIGHBOUR AS OURSELVES IS SUCH A TRUTH FOR REGULATING HUMAN SOCIETY, THAT BY THAT ALONE ONE MIGHT DETERMINE ALL THE CASES IN SOCIAL MORALITY."

"PARENTS WONDER WHY THE STREAMS ARE BITTER, WHEN THEY THEMSELVES HAVE POISONED THE FOUNTAIN."

"IT IS EASIER FOR A TUTOR TO COMMAND THAN TO TEACH."

"I ATTRIBUTE THE LITTLE I KNOW TO MY NOT HAVING BEEN ASHAMED TO ASK FOR INFORMATION, AND TO MY RULE OF CONVERSING WITH ALL DESCRIPTIONS OF MEN ON THOSE TOPICS THAT FORM THEIR OWN PECULIAR PROFESSIONS AND PURSUITS."

"I HAVE SPENT MORE THAN HALF A LIFETIME TRYING TO EXPRESS THE TRAGIC MOMENT."

"FORTITUDE IS THE GUARD AND SUPPORT OF THE OTHER VIRTUES."

"WE SHOULD HAVE A GREAT FEWER DISPUTES IN THE WORLD IF WORDS WERE TAKEN FOR WHAT THEY ARE, THE SIGNS OF OUR IDEAS ONLY, AND NOT FOR THINGS THEMSELVES."

"THINGS OF THIS WORLD ARE IN SO CONSTANT A FLUX, THAT NOTHING REMAINS LONG IN THE SAME STATE."

"THE DISCIPLINE OF DESIRE IS THE BACKGROUND OF CHARACTER."

"IT IS ONE THING TO SHOW A MAN THAT HE IS IN AN ERROR, AND ANOTHER TO PUT HIM IN POSSESSION OF THE TRUTH."

"ONE UNERRING MARK OF THE LOVE OF TRUTH IS NOT ENTERTAINING ANY PROPOSITION WITH GREATER ASSURANCE THAN THE PROOFS IT IS BUILT UPON WILL WARRANT."

"OUR DEEDS DISGUISE US. PEOPLE NEED ENDLESS TIME TO TRY ON THEIR DEEDS, UNTIL EACH KNOWS THE PROPER DEEDS FOR HIM TO DO. BUT EVERY DAY, EVERY HOUR, RUSHES BY. THERE IS NO TIME."

"ANYONE REFLECTING UPON THE THOUGHT HE HAS OF THE DELIGHT, WHICH ANY PRESENT OR ABSENT THING IS APT TO PRODUCE IN HIM, HAS THE IDEA WE CALL LOVE."

"FASHION FOR THE MOST PART IS NOTHING BUT THE OSTENTATION OF RICHES."

"MAN... HATH BY NATURE A POWER .... TO PRESERVE HIS PROPERTY - THAT IS, HIS LIFE, LIBERTY, AND ESTATE - AGAINST THE INJURIES AND ATTEMPTS OF OTHER MEN."

"NATURE NEVER MAKES EXCELLENT THINGS FOR MEAN OR NO USES."

"NOBODY IS GOING TO LET ANYBODY'S CHILDREN PLAY ON SOMETHING THAT IS UNSAFE. THERE IS JUST NO WAY."

"OUR SAVIOUR'S GREAT RULE, THAT WE SHOULD LOVE OUR NEIGHBOURS AS OURSELVES, IS SUCH A FUNDAMENTAL TRUTH FOR THE REGULATING OF HUMAN SOCIETY, THAT, BY THAT ALONE, ONE MIGHT WITHOUT DIFFICULTY DETERMINE ALL THE CASES AND DOUBTS IN SOCIAL MORALITY."

"THERE BEING NOTHING MORE EVIDENT THAN THAT CREATURES OF THE SAME SPECIES SHOULD BE EQUAL AMONGST ONE ANOTHER WITHOUT SUBORDINATION OR SUBJECTION."

"IT IS SO VITAL TO EVERYBODY WHO HAS A STAKE IN THE DOWNTOWN. IT IS VITAL TO ANYONE WHO LIVES HERE. IT IS GOING TO PUT US ON THE MAP."

"IF PUNISHMENT MAKES NOT THE WILL SUPPLE IT HARDENS THE OFFENDER."

SIMPLY PHILOSOPHICAL QUOTES

"THE GREAT QUESTION ABOUT POWER IS WHO SHOULD HAVE IT."

"HE WOULD BE LAUGHED AT, THAT SHOULD GO ABOUT TO MAKE A FINE DANCER OUT OF A COUNTRY HEDGER, AT PAST FIFTY. AND HE WILL NOT HAVE MUCH BETTER SUCCESS, WHO SHALL ENDEAVOUR, AT THAT AGE, TO MAKE A MAN REASON WELL, OR SPEAK HANDSOMELY, WHO HAS NEVER BEEN USED TO IT, THOUGH YOU SHOULD LAY BEFORE HIM A COLLECTION OF ALL THE BEST PRECEPTS OF LOGIC OR ORATORY."

"SOME EYES WANT SPECTACLES TO SEE THINGS CLEARLY AND DISTINCTLY: BUT LET NOT THOSE THAT USE THEM THEREFORE SAY NOBODY CAN SEE CLEARLY WITHOUT THEM."

"THE NEXT THING IS BY GENTLE DEGREES TO ACCUSTOM CHILDREN TO THOSE THINGS THEY ARE TOO AFRAID OF. BUT HERE GREAT CAUTION IS TO BE USED, THAT YOU DO NOT MAKE TOO MUCH HASTE, NOR ATTEMPT THIS CURE TOO EARLY, FOR FEAR LEST YOU INCREASE THE MISCHIEF INSTEAD OF REMEDYING IT."

"UNTRUTH BEING UNACCEPTABLE TO THE MIND OF MAN, THERE IS NO OTHER DEFENCE LEFT FOR ABSURDITY BUT OBSCURITY."

"THERE IS NOT SO CONTEMPTIBLE A PLANT OR ANIMAL THAT DOES NOT CONFOUND THE MOST ENLARGED UNDERSTANDING."

"ALL MEN BY NATURE ARE EQUAL IN THAT EQUAL RIGHT THAT EVERY MAN HATH TO HIS NATURAL FREEDOM, WITHOUT BEING SUBJECTED TO THE WILL OR AUTHORITY OF ANY OTHER MAN; BEING ALL EQUAL AND INDEPENDENT, NO ONE OUGHT TO HARM ANOTHER IN HIS LIFE, HEALTH, LIBERTY OR POSSESSIONS."

"MEMORY IS THE POWER TO REVIVE AGAIN IN OUR MINDS THOSE IDEAS WHICH AFTER IMPRINTING HAVE DISAPPEARED, OR HAVE BEEN LAID ASIDE OUT OF SIGHT."

"LIBERTY IS TO BE FREE FROM RESTRAINT AND VIOLENCE FROM OTHERS."

"IT IS LABOUR INDEED THAT PUTS THE DIFFERENCE ON EVERYTHING."

"NOTHING IS IN THE INTELLECT THAT WAS NOT FIRST IN THE SENSES."

"SINCE THE GREAT FOUNDATION OF FEAR IS PAIN, THE WAY TO HARDEN AND FORTIFY CHILDREN AGAINST FEAR AND DANGER IS TO ACCUSTOM THEM TO SUFFER PAIN."

"CURIOSITY SHOULD BE AS CAREFULLY CHERISHED IN CHILDREN, AS OTHER APPETITES SUPPRESSED."

"IT IS AMBITION ENOUGH TO BE EMPLOYED AS AN UNDER-LABOURER IN CLEARING THE GROUND A LITTLE, AND REMOVING SOME OF THE RUBBISH THAT LIES IN THE WAY TO KNOWLEDGE."

"TO BE RATIONAL IS SO GLORIOUS A THING, THAT TWO-LEGGED CREATURES GENERALLY CONTENT THEMSELVES WITH THE TITLE."

"IF ALL BE A DREAM, THEN HE DOTH BUT DREAM THAT HE MAKES THE QUESTION; AND SO IT IS NOT MUCH MATTER THAT A WAKING MAN SHOULD ANSWER HIM."

"AS MUCH LAND AS A MAN TILLS, PLANTS, IMPROVES, CULTIVATED, AND CAN USE THE PRODUCT OF, SO MUCH IS HIS PROPERTY. HE BY HIS LABOUR DOES, AS IT WERE, ENCLOSE IT FROM THE COMMON."

"IT IS VAIN TO FIND FAULT WITH THOSE ARTS OF DECEIVING WHEREIN MEN FIND PLEASURE TO BE DECEIVED."

"TILL A MAN CAN JUDGE WHETHER THEY BE TRUTHS OR NOT, HIS UNDERSTANDING IS BUT LITTLE IMPROVED, AND THUS MEN OF MUCH READING, THOUGH GREATLY LEARNED, BUT MAY BE LITTLE KNOWING."

"IS IT WORTH THE NAME OF FREEDOM TO BE AT LIBERTY TO PLAY THE FOOL?"

"HE THAT THINKS ABSOLUTE POWER PURIFIES MEN'S BLOOD, AND CORRECTS THE BASENESS OF HUMAN NATURE, NEEDS ONLY TO READ THE HISTORY OF THIS, OR ANY OTHER AGE, TO BE CONVINCED TO THE CONTRARY."

"SET THE MIND TO WORK, AND APPLY THE THOUGHTS VIGOROUSLY TO THE BUSINESS, FOR IT HOLDS IN THE STRUGGLES OF THE MIND, AS IN THOSE OF WAR, THAT TO THINK WE SHALL CONQUER IS TO CONQUER."

"THESE TWO, I SAY, EXTERNAL MATERIAL THINGS, AS THE OBJECTS OF SENSATION AND THE OPERATIONS OF OUR OWN MINDS WITHIN, AS THE OBJECTS OF REFLECTION, ARE TO ME THE ONLY ORIGINALS FROM WHENCE ALL OUR IDEAS TAKE THEIR BEGINNINGS."

"FIRMNESS OR STIFFNESS OF THE MIND IS NOT FROM ADHERENCE TO TRUTH, BUT SUBMISSION TO PREJUDICE."

"ERROR IS NONE THE BETTER FOR BEING COMMON, NOR TRUTH THE WORSE FOR HAVING LAIN NEGLECTED."

"ANGER IS UNEASINESS OR DISCOMPOSURE OF THE MIND UPON THE RECEIPT OF ANY INJURY, WITH A PRESENT PURPOSE OF REVENGE."

"KNOWLEDGE BEING TO BE HAD ONLY OF VISIBLE AND CERTAIN TRUTH, ERROR IS NOT A FAULT OF OUR KNOWLEDGE, BUT A MISTAKE OF OUR JUDGMENT, GIVING ASSENT TO THAT WHICH IS NOT TRUE."

"CHILDREN GENERALLY HATE TO BE IDLE; ALL THE CARE THEN IS THAT THEIR BUSY HUMOUR SHOULD BE CONSTANTLY EMPLOYED IN SOMETHING OF USE TO THEM."

"CERTAIN SUBJECTS YIELD A GENERAL POWER THAT MAY BE APPLIED IN ANY DIRECTION AND SHOULD BE STUDIED BY ALL."

"HENCE IT IS A MISTAKE TO THINK THAT
THE SUPREME OR LEGISLATIVE POWER OF
ANY COMMON-WEALTH, CAN DO WHAT IT
WILL, AND DISPOSE OF THE ESTATES OF THE
SUBJECT ARBITRARILY, OR TAKE ANY PART
OF THEM AT PLEASURE."

"THE CHURCH WHICH TAUGHT MEN NOT TO
KEEP FAITH WITH HERETICS, HAD NO CLAIM
TO TOLERATION."

"FAITH IS THE ASSENT TO ANY PROPOSITION
NOT MADE OUT BY THE DEDUCTION OF
REASON BUT UPON THE CREDIT OF THE
PROPOSER."

"THERE ARE TWO SIDES, TWO PLAYERS. ONE
IS LIGHT, THE OTHER IS DARK."

"WITH BOOKS WE STAND ON THE
SHOULDERS OF GIANTS."

"WHEN WE KNOW OUR OWN STRENGTH, WE SHALL THE BETTER KNOW WHAT TO UNDERTAKE WITH HOPES OF SUCCESS…"

"DON'T LET THE THINGS YOU DON'T HAVE PREVENT YOU FROM USING WHAT YOU DO HAVE."

"THAT WHICH PARENTS SHOULD TAKE CARE OF… IS TO DISTINGUISH BETWEEN THE WANTS OF FANCY, AND THOSE OF NATURE."

"AND THUS THE COMMUNITY PERPETUALLY RETAINS A SUPREME POWER OF SAVING THEMSELVES FROM THE ATTEMPTS AND DESIGNS OF ANYBODY, EVEN OF THEIR LEGISLATORS, WHENEVER THEY SHALL BE SO FOOLISH, OR SO WICKED, AS TO LAY AND CARRY ON DESIGNS AGAINST THE LIBERTIES AND PROPERTIES OF THE SUBJECT."

"BOOKS SEEM TO ME TO BE PESTILENT THINGS, AND INFECT ALL THAT TRADE IN THEM...WITH SOMETHING VERY PERVERSE AND BRUTAL. PRINTERS, BINDERS, SELLERS, AND OTHERS THAT MAKE A TRADE AND GAIN OUT OF THEM HAVE UNIVERSALLY SO ODD A TURN AND CORRUPTION OF MIND THAT THEY HAVE A WAY OF DEALING PECULIAR TO THEMSELVES, AND NOT CONFORMED TO THE GOOD OF SOCIETY AND THAT GENERAL FAIRNESS WHICH CEMENTS MANKIND."

"THE GREAT ART TO LEARN MUCH IS TO UNDERTAKE A LITTLE AT A TIME."

SIDDĀRTHA GAUTAMA

*A*t a point between the 6-4th century BC, Siddhartha Gautama was born in Lumbini, present-day Nepal. He would go on to become 'the enlightened one' and thus the Buddha, founder of Buddhism. It was prophesied that he would either become the emperor of India, or a very holy man. He grew up as a prince living in bliss, protected from the misfortunes and troubles of the outside world. When he left the comfort of his abundant household, he was astounded to find the happenings and harsh realities around him, sickness, poverty and death among them. Eventually, he left his palace for good and was inspired by a holy man to go and seek enlightenment - freedom from suffering. Six years later, he finally found it. At some point, his wandering brought him to a tree that stood out to him. Meditating under it, he found enlightenment and saw the world from afar and his past lives, and understood the cycle of life, death and rebirth. He gained supreme wisdom and from then on, he became the Buddha or the 'awakened one' and was called Shakyamuni Buddha. This is how Buddhism was formed as a religion, although the king Ashoka spreading the word around Asia, a couple of centuries after the Buddha's death, is a big part of it becoming the size it is today.

The Buddha taught well into his old age, dying at around 80 years old. This came shortly after he was offered a meal by a blacksmith named Cunda, but it was found that the cause of death was not food poisoning, but rather mesenteric root syndrome, a symptom of old age. The Buddha instructed his attendant to inform the blacksmith that his meal would be a source of the greatest merit as it would be the Buddha's last meal. After the body was cremated, the remains including bones were distributed as relics around various north Indian kingdoms.

Moderation

One shouldn't bathe in luxury. The Buddha discovered that the thing that connects all of creation, be it a distraught ant or dying human, is suffering. At the same time, one should not abstain from comfort whatsoever but instead, live in moderation. This is 'madhyamā-pratipad' or 'the middle way'.

Managing Attachment

Attachment is the root of all suffering, and therefore we can transcend suffering by managing or removing our desires. The Buddha taught that we must look to change our outlook over our circumstances and that the reason people are unhappy is because they are greedy, insecure and vain. With change in the mind, one can become content.

Cause and Effect

The Buddha taught that we receive exactly what we earn, whether that is good or bad. This way, our thoughts and actions determine our life. This, of course, is called karma and in this way, science and Buddhism share similarities, as the law of cause and effect is accepted in modern science.

5 Facts About The Buddha

1. The *Mahaparinibbana Sutta,* a scripture regarding the end of Siddhartha Gautama's life, depicts him saying he cannot promote anyone to be his successor.
2. The Buddha is often depicted as chubby but this was actually not the case, the reason for this portrayal is because it was symbolic of happiness in the middle east.
3. The Buddha's spot of enlightenment underneath the bodhi tree is still preserved today. The bodhi tree is a symbol of Buddhism.
4. At the time, most monastic orders did not allow females to participate; as one might expect, society in the middle east was very male-dominated. The Buddha was a contrast of this and treated females equally.
5. The Buddha had no interest in gods, he believed they were not relevant to the goal of enlightenment. Buddhism is the only main religion today with no gods.

88 BUDDHA QUOTES

"DO NOT DWELL IN THE PAST, DO NOT DREAM OF THE FUTURE, CONCENTRATE THE MIND ON THE PRESENT MOMENT."

"THE SECRET OF HEALTH FOR BOTH MIND AND BODY IS NOT TO MOURN FOR THE PAST, NOR TO WORRY ABOUT THE FUTURE, BUT TO LIVE THE PRESENT MOMENT WISELY AND EARNESTLY."

"EVERY MORNING WE ARE BORN AGAIN. WHAT WE DO TODAY IS WHAT MATTERS MOST."

"BE WHERE YOU ARE; OTHERWISE YOU WILL MISS YOUR LIFE."

"WHAT YOU ARE IS WHAT YOU HAVE BEEN. WHAT YOU'LL BE IS WHAT YOU DO NOW."

"IT IS BETTER TO TRAVEL WELL THAN TO ARRIVE."

"NO ONE SAVES US BUT OURSELVES. NO ONE CAN AND NO ONE MAY. WE OURSELVES MUST WALK THE PATH."

"A MAN IS NOT CALLED WISE BECAUSE HE TALKS AND TALKS AGAIN; BUT IF HE IS PEACEFUL, LOVING AND FEARLESS THEN HE IS IN TRUTH CALLED WISE."

"PURITY OR IMPURITY DEPENDS ON ONESELF, NO ONE CAN PURIFY ANOTHER."

"JUST AS A SNAKE SHEDS ITS SKIN, WE MUST SHED OUR PAST OVER AND OVER AGAIN."

"PEACE COMES FROM WITHIN. DO NOT SEEK IT WITHOUT."

"WHAT IS EVIL? KILLING IS EVIL, LYING IS EVIL, SLANDERING IS EVIL, ABUSE IS EVIL, GOSSIP IS EVIL, ENVY IS EVIL, HATRED IS EVIL, TO CLING TO FALSE DOCTRINE IS EVIL; ALL THESE THINGS ARE EVIL. AND WHAT IS THE ROOT OF EVIL? DESIRE IS THE ROOT OF EVIL, ILLUSION IS THE ROOT OF EVIL."

"TO INSIST ON A SPIRITUAL PRACTICE THAT SERVED YOU IN THE PAST IS TO CARRY THE RAFT ON YOUR BACK AFTER YOU HAVE CROSSED THE RIVER."

"IF YOU FIND NO ONE TO SUPPORT YOU ON THE SPIRITUAL PATH, WALK ALONE."

"THE ONE IN WHOM NO LONGER EXISTS THE CRAVING AND THIRST THAT PERPETUATE BECOMING; HOW COULD YOU TRACK THAT AWAKENED ONE, TRACKLESS, AND OF LIMITLESS RANGE."

"ENDURANCE IS ONE OF THE MOST
DIFFICULT DISCIPLINES, BUT IT IS TO THE
ONE WHO ENDURES THAT THE FINAL
VICTORY COMES."

"WHEN YOU REALISE HOW PERFECT
EVERYTHING IS YOU WILL TILT YOUR HEAD
BACK AND LAUGH AT THE SKY."

"THE FOOT FEELS THE FOOT WHEN IT FEELS
THE GROUND."

"ANGER WILL NEVER DISAPPEAR SO LONG AS
THOUGHTS OF RESENTMENT ARE
CHERISHED IN THE MIND."

"TRUE LOVE IS BORN FROM
UNDERSTANDING."

"YOU, YOURSELF, AS MUCH AS ANYBODY IN
THE ENTIRE UNIVERSE, DESERVE YOUR
LOVE AND AFFECTION."

"YOU ONLY LOSE WHAT YOU CLING TO."

"RADIATE BOUNDLESS LOVE TOWARDS THE ENTIRE WORLD."

"AMBITION IS LIKE LOVE, IMPATIENT BOTH OF DELAYS AND RIVALS."

"LOVE IS A GIFT OF ONE'S INNERMOST SOUL TO ANOTHER SO BOTH CAN BE WHOLE."

"HATRED DOES NOT CEASE BY HATRED, BUT ONLY BY LOVE; THIS IS THE ETERNAL RULE."

"JUST AS A MOTHER WOULD PROTECT HER ONLY CHILD WITH HER LIFE, EVEN SO LET ONE CULTIVATE A BOUNDLESS LOVE TOWARDS ALL BEINGS."

"THERE IS NOTHING SO DISOBEDIENT AS AN UNDISCIPLINED MIND, AND THERE IS NOTHING SO OBEDIENT AS A DISCIPLINED MIND."

"OUR LIFE IS SHAPED BY OUR THOUGHTS;
WE BECOME WHAT WE THINK. WHEN THE
MIND IS PURE, JOY FOLLOWS LIKE A
SHADOW THAT NEVER LEAVES. SUFFERING
FOLLOWS AN EVIL THOUGHT AS THE
WHEELS OF A CART FOLLOW THE OXEN THAT
DRAWS IT."

"WHATEVER A MONK KEEPS PURSUING WITH
HIS THINKING AND PONDERING, THAT
BECOMES THE INCLINATION OF HIS
AWARENESS."

"NOTHING CAN HARM YOU AS MUCH AS
YOUR OWN THOUGHTS UNGUARDED."

"IN THE SKY, THERE IS NO DISTINCTION OF
EAST AND WEST; PEOPLE CREATE
DISTINCTIONS OUT OF THEIR OWN MINDS
AND THEN BELIEVE THEM TO BE TRUE."

"REMEMBERING A WRONG IS LIKE CARRYING
A BURDEN ON THE MIND."

"HOLDING ON TO ANGER IS LIKE GRASPING A HOT COAL WITH THE INTENT OF THROWING IT AT SOMEONE ELSE; YOU ARE THE ONE WHO GETS BURNED."

"CHAOS IS INHERENT IN ALL COMPOUNDED THINGS. STRIVE ON WITH DILIGENCE."

"IF YOUR COMPASSION DOES NOT INCLUDE YOURSELF, IT IS INCOMPLETE."

"THOUSANDS OF CANDLES CAN BE LIT FROM A SINGLE CANDLE, AND THE LIFE OF THE CANDLE WILL NOT BE SHORTENED. HAPPINESS NEVER DECREASES BY BEING SHARED."

"AS RAIN FALLS EQUALLY ON THE JUST AND THE UNJUST, DO NOT BURDEN YOUR HEART WITH JUDGEMENT BUT RAIN YOUR KINDNESS EQUALLY ON ALL."

"A GENEROUS HEART, KIND SPEECH, AND A LIFE OF SERVICE AND COMPASSION ARE THE THINGS WHICH RENEW HUMANITY."

"IF WE FAIL TO LOOK AFTER OTHERS WHEN THEY NEED HELP, WHO WILL LOOK AFTER US?"

"HAPPINESS COMES WHEN YOUR WORK AND WORDS ARE OF BENEFIT TO OTHERS."

"GIVE, EVEN IF YOU ONLY HAVE A LITTLE."

"YOU WILL NOT BE PUNISHED FOR YOUR ANGER, YOU WILL BE PUNISHED BY YOUR ANGER."

"LIFE IS SO VERY DIFFICULT. HOW CAN WE BE ANYTHING BUT KIND?"

"WE WILL DEVELOP AND CULTIVATE THE LIBERATION OF MIND BY LOVING KINDNESS, MAKE IT OUR VEHICLE, MAKE IT OUR BASIS, STABILISE IT, EXERCISE OURSELVES IN IT, AND FULLY PERFECT IT."

"BETTER THAN A THOUSAND HOLLOW WORDS, IS ONE WORD THAT BRINGS PEACE."

"WHATEVER WORDS WE UTTER SHOULD BE CHOSEN WITH CARE FOR PEOPLE WILL HEAR THEM AND BE INFLUENCED BY THEM FOR GOOD OR ILL."

"THE TONGUE LIKE A SHARP KNIFE KILLS WITHOUT DRAWING BLOOD."

"BETTER THAN A THOUSAND HOLLOW WORDS IS ONE WORD THAT BRINGS PEACE."

"IF YOU PROPOSE TO SPEAK, ALWAYS ASK YOURSELF; IS IT TRUE, IS IT NECESSARY, IS IT KIND."

"LIKE A FINE FLOWER, BEAUTIFUL TO LOOK AT BUT WITHOUT SCENT, FINE WORDS ARE FRUITLESS IN A MAN WHO DOES NOT ACT IN ACCORDANCE WITH THEM."

"SPEAK ONLY ENDEARING SPEECH, SPEECH THAT IS WELCOMED. SPEECH, WHEN IT BRINGS NO EVIL TO OTHERS, IS A PLEASANT THING."

"THERE IS NOTHING MORE DREADFUL THAN THE HABIT OF DOUBT. DOUBT SEPARATES PEOPLE. IT IS A POISON THAT DISINTEGRATES FRIENDSHIPS AND BREAKS UP PLEASANT RELATIONS. IT IS A THORN THAT IRRITATES AND HURTS; IT IS A SWORD THAT KILLS."

"EVEN AS A SOLID ROCK IS UNSHAKEN BY THE WIND, SO ARE THE WISE UNSHAKEN BY PRAISE OR BLAME."

"AN IDEA THAT IS DEVELOPED AND PUT INTO ACTION IS MORE IMPORTANT THAN AN IDEA THAT EXISTS ONLY AS AN IDEA."

"BELIEVE NOTHING, NO MATTER WHERE
YOU READ IT, OR WHO SAID IT, NO MATTER
IF I HAVE SAID IT, UNLESS IT AGREES WITH
YOUR OWN REASON AND YOUR OWN
COMMON SENSE."

"IF YOU DO NOT CHANGE DIRECTION, YOU
MAY END UP WHERE YOU ARE HEADING."

"JUST AS THE GREAT OCEAN HAS ONE TASTE,
THE TASTE OF SALT, SO ALSO THIS
TEACHING AND DISCIPLINE HAS ONE TASTE,
THE TASTE OF LIBERATION."

"LONG IS THE NIGHT TO HIM WHO IS
AWAKE; LONG IS A MILE TO HIM WHO IS
TIRED; LONG IS LIFE TO THE FOOLISH WHO
DO NOT KNOW THE TRUE LAW."

"OUR THEORIES OF THE ETERNAL ARE AS
VALUABLE AS THOSE WHICH A CHICK
WHICH HAS NOT BROKEN ITS WAY
THROUGH ITS SHELL MIGHT FORM OF THE
OUTSIDE WORLD."

"PAIN IS CERTAIN, SUFFERING IS
OPTIONAL."

"HAVE COMPASSION FOR ALL BEINGS, RICH
AND POOR ALIKE; EACH HAS THEIR
SUFFERING. SOME SUFFER TOO MUCH,
OTHERS TOO LITTLE."

"DOUBT EVERYTHING. FIND YOUR OWN
LIGHT."

"IF YOU TRULY LOVED YOURSELF, YOU
COULD NEVER HURT ANOTHER."

"DO NOT LOOK FOR A SANCTUARY IN
ANYONE EXCEPT YOURSELF."

"THERE IS NO FIRE LIKE PASSION, THERE IS
NO SHARK LIKE HATRED, THERE IS NO
SNARE LIKE FOLLY, THERE IS NO TORRENT
LIKE GREED."

"SET YOUR HEART ON DOING GOOD. DO IT OVER AND OVER AGAIN, AND YOU WILL BE FILLED WITH JOY."

"MOST PROBLEMS, IF YOU GIVE THEM ENOUGH TIME AND SPACE, WILL EVENTUALLY WEAR THEMSELVES OUT."

"IRRIGATORS CHANNEL WATERS; FLETCHERS STRAIGHTEN ARROWS; CARPENTERS BEND WOOD; THE WISE MASTER THEMSELVES."

"DROP BY DROP IS THE WATER POT FILLED. LIKEWISE, THE WISE MAN, GATHERING IT LITTLE BY LITTLE, FILLS HIMSELF WITH GOOD."

"YOUR WORK IS TO DISCOVER YOUR WORLD AND THEN WITH ALL YOUR HEART GIVE YOURSELF TO IT."

"SHE WHO KNOWS LIFE FLOWS, FEELS NO WEAR OR TEAR, NEEDS NO MENDING OR REPAIR."

"I AM THE MIRACLE."

"LET US RISE UP AND BE THANKFUL, FOR IF WE DIDN'T LEARN A LOT AT LEAST WE LEARNED A LITTLE, AND IF WE DIDN'T LEARN A LITTLE, AT LEAST WE DIDN'T GET SICK, AND IF WE GOT SICK, AT LEAST WE DIDN'T DIE; SO, LET US ALL BE THANKFUL."

"THE WAY IS NOT IN THE SKY. THE WAY IS IN THE HEART."

"TO LIVE A PURE UNSELFISH LIFE, ONE MUST COUNT NOTHING AS ONE'S OWN IN THE MIDST OF ABUNDANCE."

"THERE IS NO FEAR FOR ONE WHOSE MIND IS NOT FILLED WITH DESIRES."

"MEDITATE... DO NOT DELAY, LEST YOU LATER REGRET IT."

226

"ARDENTLY DO TODAY WHAT MUST BE DONE. WHO KNOWS? TOMORROW, DEATH COMES."

"LIVE EVERY ACT FULLY, AS IF IT WERE YOUR LAST."

"TO BE IDLE IS A SHORT ROAD TO DEATH AND TO BE DILIGENT IS A WAY OF LIFE; FOOLISH PEOPLE ARE IDLE, WISE PEOPLE ARE DILIGENT."

"ONE WHO ACTS ON TRUTH IS HAPPY IN THIS WORLD AND BEYOND."

"A MAN ASKED GAUTAMA BUDDHA, 'I WANT HAPPINESS.' BUDDHA SAID, 'FIRST REMOVE I, THAT'S EGO, THEN REMOVE WANT, THAT'S DESIRE. SEE NOW YOU ARE LEFT WITH ONLY HAPPINESS.'"

"TO SUPPORT MOTHER AND FATHER, TO CHERISH WIFE AND CHILD AND TO HAVE A SIMPLE LIVELIHOOD; THIS IS GOOD LUCK."

"AN INSINCERE AND EVIL FRIEND IS MORE TO BE FEARED THAN A WILD BEAST; A WILD BEAST MAY WOUND YOUR BODY, BUT AN EVIL FRIEND WILL WOUND YOUR MIND."

"SHOULD A SEEKER NOT FIND A COMPANION WHO IS BETTER OR EQUAL, LET THEM RESOLUTELY PURSUE A SOLITARY COURSE."

"HE WHO LOVES 50 PEOPLE HAS 50 WOES; HE WHO LOVES NO ONE HAS NO WOES."

"ONE IS NOT CALLED NOBLE WHO HARMS LIVING BEINGS. BY NOT HARMING LIVING BEINGS ONE IS CALLED NOBLE."

EPICTETUS

$\mathcal{E}$pictetus was a Greek philosopher who was born circa 50 AD, in Hierapolis - now Pamukkale, in Turkey. He was born a slave and grew up in Rome enslaved to the secretary of the Emperor Nero, an unlikely beginning for one of the greatest philosophers whose wisdom has stood the test of time; his owner, Epaphroditus, gave him permission to pursue liberal studies, which eventually led to him becoming a student of the Stoic Gaius Musonius Rufus. Following Nero's death in 68 AD, Epictetus was freed and went on to teach philosophy in Rome, his credibility assured by his mentor. This came to an abrupt end in 93 AD, when Emperor Domitian famously banished all philosophers from Rome. Epictetus spent the rest of his life in Nicopolis in Greece where he founded a school of philosophy and taught there until his death.

Naturally, as a student of Musonius Rufus, Epictetus was a believer and practitioner of Stoicism, a philosophy of personal ethics which can be traced as far back as 300 BC, founded by the Hellenistic philosopher Zeno of Citium. The 4 virtues of Stoicism are wisdom, courage, justice, and moderation. What's fascinating about this philosophy is that three of its most renowned practitioners, Epictetus, Roman Emperor Marcus Aurelius and Seneca, advisor to an emperor as well as a playwright and of the richest people in the Roman Empire. They were born worlds apart in social status, in fact, there were no greater extremes in social status at the time than a slave and an emperor. The significance of this is it demonstrates the power of Stoicism, providing principles that do not discriminate and prove impactful, no matter where the person stands in life.

Acceptance

The importance of distinguishing what is and what isn't under our control. There are many things that are out of our control and we must let go and accept them for what they are, rather than allowing them to bring out negative emotions like anger and sadness. This also works, on the other hand, as a reminder that our actions, choices, words and emotions are all things that are in our control.

Leading With Actions

Actions speak louder than words, and one must set the example of how to be - the greatest leaders rarely speak of how things should be done, but rather their actions are what leads.

Conforming to a Character

Epictetus knew and taught that we as humans are creatures of habit and spend most of our lives acting accordingly, because of the character of ourselves we have in our heads - this leads to a tendency for us to think the ways we have are set in stone. Consequently, Epictetus advised his students to set themselves a set of principles and standards and not deviate from them, as a matter of general life. Although this requires active effort and discipline, it is what brings us closer to the character we wish to be or to embody the personal qualities we would aspire to have.

5 Facts About Epictetus

1. Epictetus never actually wrote anything; his teachings have lasted through time because of his student Arrian scribing his wisdom.
2. *Discourses* is a series of eight books consisting of Epictetus's teachings written down by Arrian, on a diverse range of subjects such as poverty, illness and anger. However, only four of the eight remain extant.
3. Albert Ellis, the psychologist who founded Cognitive Behavioural Therapy, was influenced by Epictetus.
4. Celsus, a younger contemporary of Epictetus, recounted that Epaphroditus once tortured Epictetus by twisting his leg. Epictetus endured it with patience, warning his master that his leg would break. When it did, he told Epaphroditus "Did I not tell you it would break?". As a result, he was crippled for life.
5. In his old age, he adopted a friend's child who would have been otherwise left to die.

82 EPICTETUS QUOTES

"THE KEY IS TO KEEP COMPANY ONLY WITH PEOPLE WHO UPLIFT YOU, WHOSE PRESENCE CALLS FORTH YOUR BEST."

"IS FREEDOM ANYTHING ELSE THAN THE RIGHT TO LIVE AS WE WISH? NOTHING ELSE."

"KNOW, FIRST, WHO YOU ARE, AND THEN ADORN YOURSELF ACCORDINGLY."

"WE SHOULD NOT MOOR A SHIP WITH ONE ANCHOR, OR OUR LIFE WITH ONE HOPE."

"IT'S NOT WHAT HAPPENS TO YOU, BUT HOW YOU REACT TO IT THAT MATTERS."

"IT TAKES MORE THAN JUST A GOOD LOOKING BODY. YOU'VE GOT TO HAVE THE HEART AND SOUL TO GO WITH IT."

"THE PEOPLE HAVE A RIGHT TO THE TRUTH AS THEY HAVE A RIGHT TO LIFE, LIBERTY AND THE PURSUIT OF HAPPINESS."

"KEEP SILENCE FOR THE MOST PART, AND SPEAK ONLY WHEN YOU MUST, AND THEN BRIEFLY."

"IT IS THE NATURE OF THE WISE TO RESIST PLEASURES, BUT THE FOOLISH TO BE A SLAVE TO THEM."

"IT IS IMPOSSIBLE TO BEGIN TO LEARN THAT WHICH ONE THINKS ONE ALREADY KNOWS."

"SEEK NOT GOOD FROM WITHOUT; SEEK IT WITHIN YOURSELVES, OR YOU WILL NEVER FIND IT."

"WE TELL LIES, YET IT IS EASY TO SHOW THAT LYING IS IMMORAL."

"PEOPLE ARE NOT DISTURBED BY THINGS, BUT BY THE VIEW THEY TAKE OF THEM."

"PRACTICE YOURSELF, FOR HEAVEN'S SAKE IN LITTLE THINGS, AND THEN PROCEED TO GREATER."

"IF THY BROTHER WRONGS THEE,
REMEMBER NOT SO MUCH HIS WRONG-
DOING, BUT MORE THAN EVER THAT HE IS
THY BROTHER."

"IMAGINE FOR YOURSELF A CHARACTER, A
MODEL PERSONALITY, WHOSE EXAMPLE YOU
DETERMINE TO FOLLOW, IN PRIVATE AS
WELL AS IN PUBLIC."

"NEVER IN ANY CASE SAY I HAVE LOST SUCH
A THING, BUT I HAVE RETURNED IT. IS YOUR
CHILD DEAD? IT IS A RETURN. IS YOUR WIFE
DEAD? IT IS A RETURN. ARE YOU DEPRIVED
OF YOUR ESTATE? IS THIS NOT ALSO A
RETURN?"

"THERE IS ONLY ONE WAY TO HAPPINESS
AND THAT IS TO CEASE WORRYING ABOUT
THINGS WHICH ARE BEYOND THE POWER OF
OUR WILL."

"IF EVIL BE SPOKEN OF YOU AND IT BE TRUE,
CORRECT YOURSELF, IF IT BE A LIE, LAUGH
AT IT."

"NOTHING GREAT IS CREATED SUDDENLY, ANY MORE THAN A BUNCH OF GRAPES OR A FIG. IF YOU TELL ME THAT YOU DESIRE A FIG. I ANSWER YOU THAT THERE MUST BE TIME. LET IT FIRST BLOSSOM, THEN BEAR FRUIT, THEN RIPEN."

"BE CAREFUL TO LEAVE YOUR SONS WELL INSTRUCTED RATHER THAN RICH, FOR THE HOPES OF THE INSTRUCTED ARE BETTER THAN THE WEALTH OF THE IGNORANT."

"FIRST LEARN THE MEANING OF WHAT YOU SAY, AND THEN SPEAK."

"WEALTH CONSISTS NOT IN HAVING GREAT POSSESSIONS, BUT IN HAVING FEW WANTS."

"THE TWO POWERS WHICH IN MY OPINION CONSTITUTE A WISE MAN ARE THOSE OF BEARING AND FORBEARING."

"IF YOU WANT TO IMPROVE, BE CONTENT TO BE THOUGHT FOOLISH AND STUPID."

"NOT EVERY DIFFICULT AND DANGEROUS THING IS SUITABLE FOR TRAINING, BUT ONLY THAT WHICH IS CONDUCIVE TO SUCCESS IN ACHIEVING THE OBJECT OF OUR EFFORT."

"THE WORLD TURNS ASIDE TO LET ANY MAN PASS WHO KNOWS WHERE HE IS GOING."

"WHENEVER YOU ARE ANGRY, BE ASSURED THAT IT IS NOT ONLY A PRESENT EVIL, BUT THAT YOU HAVE INCREASED A HABIT."

"ALL RELIGIONS MUST BE TOLERATED... FOR EVERY MAN MUST GET TO HEAVEN IN HIS OWN WAY."

"HE IS A WISE MAN WHO DOES NOT GRIEVE FOR THE THINGS WHICH HE HAS NOT, BUT REJOICES FOR THOSE WHICH HE HAS."

"IF ONE OVERSTEPS THE BOUNDS OF MODERATION, THE GREATEST PLEASURES CEASE TO PLEASE."

"IF VIRTUE PROMISES HAPPINESS, PROSPERITY AND PEACE, THEN PROGRESS IN VIRTUE IS PROGRESS IN EACH OF THESE FOR TO WHATEVER POINT THE PERFECTION OF ANYTHING BRINGS US, PROGRESS IS ALWAYS AN APPROACH TOWARD IT."

"IT IS NOT DEATH OR PAIN THAT IS TO BE DREADED, BUT THE FEAR OF PAIN OR DEATH."

"IT IS NOT HE WHO REVILES OR STRIKES YOU WHO INSULTS YOU, BUT YOUR OPINION THAT THESE THINGS ARE INSULTING."

"TO ACCUSE OTHERS FOR ONE'S OWN MISFORTUNES IS A SIGN OF A LACK OF EDUCATION. TO ACCUSE ONESELF SHOWS THAT ONE'S EDUCATION HAS BEGUN. TO ACCUSE NEITHER ONESELF NOR OTHERS SHOWS THAT ONE'S EDUCATION IS COMPLETE."

"THE GREATER THE DIFFICULTY THE MORE GLORY IN SURMOUNTING IT. SKILFUL PILOTS GAIN THEIR REPUTATION FROM STORMS AND TEMPESTS."

"MAKE THE BEST USE OF WHAT IS IN YOUR POWER, AND TAKE THE REST AS IT HAPPENS."

"HE IS A DRUNKARD WHO TAKES MORE THAN THREE GLASSES THOUGH HE IS NOT DRUNK."

"YOU ARE A LITTLE SOUL CARRYING AROUND A CORPSE."

"DIFFICULTIES ARE THINGS THAT SHOW A PERSON WHAT THEY ARE."

"THERE IS NOTHING GOOD OR EVIL SAVE IN THE WILL."

"YOU MAY BE ALWAYS VICTORIOUS IF YOU WILL NEVER ENTER INTO ANY CONTEST WHERE THE ISSUE DOES NOT WHOLLY DEPEND UPON YOURSELF."

"ALL PHILOSOPHY LIES IN TWO WORDS, SUSTAIN AND ABSTAIN."

"DO NOT SEEK TO BRING THINGS TO PASS IN ACCORDANCE WITH YOUR WISHES, BUT WISH FOR THEM AS THEY ARE, AND YOU WILL FIND THEM."

"IF YOU SEEK TRUTH YOU WILL NOT SEEK VICTORY BY DISHONOURABLE MEANS, AND IF YOU FIND TRUTH YOU WILL BECOME INVINCIBLE."

"UNLESS WE PLACE OUR RELIGION AND OUR TREASURE IN THE SAME THING, RELIGION WILL ALWAYS BE SACRIFICED."

"THE ESSENCE OF PHILOSOPHY IS THAT A MAN SHOULD SO LIVE THAT HIS HAPPINESS SHALL DEPEND AS LITTLE AS POSSIBLE ON EXTERNAL THINGS."

"NO MAN IS FREE WHO IS NOT MASTER OF HIMSELF."

"WE ARE NOT TO GIVE CREDIT TO THE MANY, WHO SAY THAT NONE OUGHT TO BE EDUCATED BUT THE FREE; BUT RATHER TO THE PHILOSOPHERS, WHO SAY THAT THE WELL-EDUCATED ALONE ARE FREE."

"IF YOU WISH TO BE A WRITER, WRITE."

"WHEN YOU ARE OFFENDED AT ANY MAN'S FAULT, TURN TO YOURSELF AND STUDY YOUR OWN FAILINGS. THEN YOU WILL FORGET YOUR ANGER."

"WHOEVER DOES NOT REGARD WHAT HE HAS AS MOST AMPLE WEALTH, IS UNHAPPY, THOUGH HE BE MASTER OF THE WORLD."

"FREEDOM IS NOT PROCURED BY A FULL
ENJOYMENT OF WHAT IS DESIRED, BUT BY
CONTROLLING THE DESIRE."

"IF YOU DESIRE TO BE GOOD, BEGIN BY
BELIEVING THAT YOU ARE WICKED."

"ONE THAT DESIRES TO EXCEL SHOULD
ENDEAVOUR IN THOSE THINGS THAT ARE IN
THEMSELVES MOST EXCELLENT."

"I HAVE A LANTERN. YOU STEAL MY
LANTERN. WHAT, THEN, IS YOUR HONOUR
WORTH NO MORE TO YOU THAN THE PRICE
OF MY LANTERN?"

"REMEMBER THAT YOU ARE AN ACTOR IN A DRAMA, OF SUCH A PART AS IT MAY PLEASE THE MASTER TO ASSIGN YOU, FOR A LONG TIME OR FOR A LITTLE AS HE MAY CHOOSE. AND IF HE WILL TAKE THE PART OF A POOR MAN, OR A CRIPPLE, OR A RULER, OR A PRIVATE CITIZEN, THEN MAY YOU ACT THAT PART WITH GRACE! FOR TO ACT WELL THE PART THAT IS ALLOTTED TO US, THAT INDEED IS OURS TO DO, BUT TO CHOOSE IT IS ANOTHER'S."

"WE MUST NOT BELIEVE THE MANY, WHO SAY THAT ONLY FREE PEOPLE OUGHT TO BE EDUCATED, BUT WE SHOULD RATHER BELIEVE THE PHILOSOPHERS WHO SAY THAT ONLY THE EDUCATED ARE FREE."

"DIFFICULTIES SHOW MEN WHAT THEY ARE. IN CASE OF ANY DIFFICULTY REMEMBER THAT GOD HAS PITTED YOU AGAINST A ROUGH ANTAGONIST THAT YOU MAY BE A CONQUEROR, AND THIS CANNOT BE WITHOUT TOIL."

"SO YOU WISH TO CONQUER IN THE OLYMPIC GAMES, MY FRIEND? AND I TOO, BY THE GODS, AND A FINE THING IT WOULD BE! BUT FIRST MARK THE CONDITIONS AND THE CONSEQUENCES, AND THEN SET TO WORK. YOU WILL HAVE TO PUT YOURSELF UNDER DISCIPLINE; TO EAT BY RULE, TO AVOID CAKES AND SWEETMEATS; TO TAKE EXERCISE AT THE APPOINTED HOUR WHETHER YOU LIKE IT OR NO, IN COLD AND HEAT; TO ABSTAIN FROM COLD DRINKS AND FROM WINE AT YOUR WILL; IN A WORD, TO GIVE YOURSELF OVER TO THE TRAINER AS TO A PHYSICIAN. THEN IN THE CONFLICT ITSELF YOU ARE LIKELY ENOUGH TO DISLOCATE YOUR WRIST OR TWIST YOUR ANKLE, TO SWALLOW A GREAT DEAL OF DUST, OR TO BE SEVERELY THRASHED, AND, AFTER ALL THESE THINGS, TO BE DEFEATED."

"A STRICT BELIEF, FATE IS THE WORST KIND OF SLAVERY; ON THE OTHER HAND THERE IS COMFORT IN THE THOUGHT THAT GOD WILL BE MOVED BY OUR PRAYERS."

"DO NOT SEEK TO HAVE EVENTS HAPPEN AS YOU WANT THEM TO, BUT INSTEAD WANT THEM TO HAPPEN AS THEY DO HAPPEN, AND YOUR LIFE WILL GO WELL."

"WHAT MATTERS MOST IS WHAT SORT OF PERSON YOU ARE BECOMING. WISE INDIVIDUALS CARE ONLY ABOUT WHOM THEY ARE TODAY AND WHO THEY CAN BE TOMORROW."

"EMBRACE REALITY. THINK ABOUT WHAT DELIGHTS YOU - THE SMALL LUXURIES ON WHICH YOU DEPEND, THE PEOPLE WHOM YOU CHERISH MOST. BUT REMEMBER THAT THEY HAVE THEIR OWN DISTINCT CHARACTER, WHICH IS QUITE A SEPARATE MATTER FROM HOW WE HAPPEN TO REGARD THEM."

"NEVER DEPEND ON THE ADMIRATION OF OTHERS FOR SELF-SATISFACTION. IT IS A FACT OF LIFE THAT OTHER PEOPLE, EVEN PEOPLE WHO LOVE YOU, WILL NOT NECESSARILY AGREE WITH YOUR IDEAS, UNDERSTAND YOU ALWAYS, OR SHARE YOUR ENTHUSIASMS."

"WHEN YOUR THOUGHTS, WORDS, AND DEEDS FORM A SEAMLESS FABRIC, YOU STREAMLINE YOUR EFFORTS AND THUS ELIMINATE WORRY AND DREAD."

"THE UNIVERSE IS BUT ONE GREAT CITY, FULL OF BELOVED ONES, DIVINE AND HUMAN, BY NATURE ENDEARED TO EACH OTHER."

"IT'S TIME TO STOP BEING VAGUE. IF YOU WISH TO BE AN EXTRAORDINARY PERSON, IF YOU WISH TO BE WISE, THEN YOU SHOULD EXPLICITLY IDENTIFY THE KIND OF PERSON YOU ASPIRE TO BECOME."

"IT IS NOT A DEMONSTRATION OF KINDNESS OR FRIENDSHIP TO THE PEOPLE WE CARE ABOUT TO JOIN THEM IN INDULGING IN WRONGHEADED, NEGATIVE FEELINGS. WE DO A BETTER SERVICE TO OURSELVES AND OTHERS BY REMAINING DETACHED AND AVOIDING MELODRAMATIC REACTIONS."

"YOU ARE BUT AN APPEARANCE, AND NOT ABSOLUTELY THE THING YOU APPEAR TO BE."

"TENTATIVE EFFORTS LEAD TO TENTATIVE OUTCOMES."

"IT IS NOT HE WHO GIVES ABUSE THAT AFFRONTS, BUT THE VIEW THAT WE TAKE OF IT AS INSULTING; SO THAT WHEN ONE PROVOKES YOU IT IS YOUR OWN OPINION WHICH IS PROVOKING."

"IN HIM WE HAVE REDEMPTION THROUGH HIS BLOOD, THE FORGIVENESS OF OUR TRESPASSES, ACCORDING TO THE RICHES OF HIS GRACE."

"NOTHING IS IN REALITY EITHER PLEASANT OR UNPLEASANT BY NATURE BUT ALL THINGS BECOME SO THROUGH HABIT."

"YOUR MASTER IS HE WHO CONTROLS THAT ON WHICH YOU HAVE SET YOUR HEART OR WISH TO AVOID."

"DON'T CONSENT TO BE HURT AND YOU WON'T BE HURT – THIS IS A CHOICE OVER WHICH YOU HAVE CONTROL."

"IF YOU HAVE ASSUMED A CHARACTER ABOVE YOUR STRENGTH, YOU HAVE BOTH ACTED IN THIS MATTER IN AN UNBECOMING WAY, AND YOU HAVE NEGLECTED THAT WHICH YOU MIGHT HAVE FULFILLED."

"EACH MAN'S LIFE IS A KIND OF CAMPAIGN, AND A LONG AND COMPLICATED ONE AT THAT. YOU HAVE TO MAINTAIN THE CHARACTER OF A SOLDIER, AND DO EACH SEPARATE ACT AT THE BIDDING OF THE GENERAL."

"NOTHING GREAT COMES INTO BEING ALL AT ONCE."

"SICKNESS IS A HINDRANCE TO THE BODY, BUT NOT TO YOUR ABILITY TO CHOOSE, UNLESS THAT IS YOUR CHOICE. LAMENESS IS A HINDRANCE TO THE LEG, BUT NOT TO YOUR ABILITY TO CHOOSE. SAY THIS TO YOURSELF WITH REGARD TO EVERYTHING THAT HAPPENS, THEN YOU WILL SEE SUCH OBSTACLES AS HINDRANCES TO SOMETHING ELSE, BUT NOT TO YOURSELF."

"NEVER LOOK FOR YOUR WORK IN ONE PLACE AND YOUR PROGRESS IN ANOTHER."

"IN THEORY IT IS EASY TO CONVINCE AN IGNORANT PERSON; IN ACTUAL LIFE, MEN NOT ONLY OBJECT TO OFFERING THEMSELVES TO BE CONVINCED, BUT HATE THE MAN WHO HAS CONVINCED THEM."

REFERENCE LIST

10 Fun Facts Every Tourist Should Know About Confucius. (2020). Retrieved 28 November 2020, from https://www.chinahighlights.com/travelguide/china-history/confucius-facts.htm

%20an%20ancient%20Chinese,Confucian%20philoso-pher%20after%20Confucius%20himself.

12 Interesting Facts About Aristotle | OhFact!. (2020). Retrieved 20 November 2020, from https://ohfact.com/aristotle-facts/

100 Famous Confucius Quotes. (2020). Retrieved 17 October 2020, from https://www.quoteambition.com/confucius-quotes/

100 Top Quotes By Friedrich Nietzsche That Smash Popular Notions. (2020). Retrieved 30 November 2020, from https://quotes.thefamouspeople.com/friedrich-nietzsche-128.php

30 Interesting Socrates Facts. (2015). Retrieved 15 November 2020, from https://factslegend.org/30-interesting-socrates-facts/

Aristotle Quotes - BrainyQuote. (2001). Retrieved 30 November 2020, from https://www.brainyquote.com/authors/aristotle-quotes

A. Watson, R., 2020. *Rene Descartes | Biography, Philosophy, & Facts.* [online] Encyclopaedia Britannica. Available at: <https://www.britannica.com/biography/Rene-Descartes> [Accessed 30 November 2020

A List of Famous Plato Quotes. (2017). Retrieved 22 November 2020, from https://www.ranker.com/list/a-list-of-famous-plato-quotes/reference

Adam, M. (2004). PHILOSOPHY - Plato. Retrieved 21 November 2020, from https://www.youtube.com/watch?v=VDiyQub6vpw

Angelah. (2020). Top 10 intriguing facts about Socrates. Retrieved 23 November 2020, from https://www.discoverwalks.com/blog/greece/top-10-intriguing-facts-about-socrates/

Baidya, S., o, j., Patel, P., Baidya, S., squid, g., Dixon, A., & fetus, Y. (2020). 30 Interesting Aristotle Facts You Should Know. Retrieved 30 November 2020, from https://factslegend.org/30-interesting-aristotle-facts-know/

Epictetus (Stanford Encyclopaedia of Philosophy). (2017). Retrieved 30 November 2020, from https://plato.stanford.edu/entries/epictetus/

Epictetus Quotes - BrainyQuote. Retrieved 30 November 2020, from https://www.brainyquote.com/authors/epictetus-quotes

Who Is Epictetus? From Slave To World's Most Sought After Philosopher. (2020). Retrieved 30 November 2020, from https://dailystoic.com/epictetus/

Epictetus | Greek philosopher. (2020). Retrieved 30 November 2020, from https://www.britannica.com/biography/Epictetus-Greek-philosopher

Friedrich Nietzsche (Stanford Encyclopaedia of Philosophy). (2017). Retrieved 30 November 2020, from https://plato.stanford.edu/entries/nietzsche/

https://www.goodreads.com/author/show/1938.Friedrich_Nietzsche

Hutyra, H. (2018). 119 Socrates Quotes That Offer A More Peaceful Way Of Life. Retrieved 21 November

2020, from https://www.keepinspiring.me/socrates-quotes/

Inspirational Quotes To Fire You Up With Motivation Even When Taking A Single Step Seems Difficult. (2020). Retrieved 15 November 2020, from https://quotes.thefamouspeople.com/aristotle-116.p

Immanuel Kant (Stanford Encyclopaedia of Philosophy). (2010). Retrieved 30 November 2020, from https://plato.stanford.edu/entries/kant/

John Locke. HISTORY. (2009). Retrieved 30 November 2020, from https://www.history.com/topics/british-history/john-locke.

John Locke | Biography, Works, & Facts. (2020). Retrieved 21 November 2020, from https://www.britannica.com/biography/John-Locke

John Locke. (2019). Retrieved 30 November 2020, from https://www.history.com/topics/british-history/john-locke

Kant's Moral Philosophy (Stanford Encyclopaedia of Philosophy). (2004). Retrieved 19 November 2020, from https://plato.stanford.edu/entries/kant-moral/

Magnus, B. (2020). Friedrich Nietzsche. Retrieved 30 November 2020, from https://www.britannica.com/biography/Friedrich-Nietzsche

Medrut, F. 25 Immanuel Kant Quotes on Pure Reason and Morality. Retrieved 17 November 2020, from https://www.goalcast.com/2019/11/21/immanuel-kant-quotes/

Meinwald, C. Plato | Life, Philosophy, & Works. Retrieved 20 November 2020, from https://www.britannica.com/biography/Plato*Locke's Political Philosophy (Stanford Encyclopaedia of Philosophy)*. Plato.stanford.edu. (2005). Retrieved 23 November 2020, from https://plato.stanford.edu/entries/locke-political/.

Medrut, F. (2018). 20 Plato Quotes to Freshen Up your Philosophy on Life. Retrieved 24 November 2020, from https://www.goalcast.com/2018/02/21/20-plato-quotes/

November 2020, from https://www.goalcast.com/2018/05/02/best-confucius-quotes-to-inspire-you

Confucius Quotes (Author of The Analects). (2020). Retrieved 13 November 2020, from https://www.goodreads.com/author/quotes/15321.Confucius

Nietzsche, F. (2020). Friedrich Nietzsche. Retrieved 30 November 2020, from https://www.goodreads.com/author/show/1938.Friedrich_Nietzsche

Plato Is Considered To Be One Of The Greatest Philosophers Ever & Here's Why. Retrieved 22

November 2020, from https://quotes.thefamouspeople.com/plato-257.php

Pittman, H. (2008). René Descartes (Stanford Encyclopaedia of Philosophy). Retrieved 14 November 2020, from https://plato.stanford.edu/entries/descartes/

Rene Descartes Quotations at QuoteTab. Retrieved 28 November 2020, from https://www.quotetab.com/quotes/by-rene-descartes

Rene Descartes Quotes - BrainyQuote. (2020). Retrieved 30 November 2020, from https://www.brainyquote.com/authors/rene-descartes-quotes

REILLY, L. (2018). 17 Things to Know About René Descartes. Retrieved 12 November 2020, from https://www.mentalfloss.com/article/550161/facts-about-rene-descartes

René Descartes (Stanford Encyclopaedia of Philosophy). (2014). Retrieved 30 November 2020, from https://plato.stanford.edu/entries/descartes/

Socrates Quotes - BrainyQuote. Retrieved 18 November 2020, from https://www.brainyquote.com/authors/socrates-quotes

Singh, G. (2019). *Buddha Quotes – 100 Breathtaking Quotes by Buddha — The Yogi Press*. The Yogi Press.

Retrieved 12 November 2020, from https://www.yogi.
press/home/buddha-quotes.

Seale, Q. (2017). 113 Aristotle Quotes That Changed
Western History Forever. Retrieved 16 November
2020, from https://www.keepinspiring.me/aristotle-
quotes/

S. Lopez, D. (2020). *Buddha | Biography, Teachings, Influ-
ence, & Facts.* Encyclopaedia Britannica. Retrieved 30
November 2020, from https://www.britannica.com/
biography/Buddha-founder-of-Buddhism

Top 10 Facts about John Locke. Discoverwalks.com.
(2020). Retrieved 18 November 2020, from https://
www.discoverwalks.com/blog/top10/top-10-facts-
about-john-locke/.

Who was Buddha? A short life story of Buddha Shakyamuni.
Diamond Way Buddhism. (2020). Retrieved 30
November 2020, from https://www.diamondway-
buddhism.org/buddhism/buddha/.

Who was Epictetus? Everything You Need to Know.
Retrieved 30 November 2020, from https://www.
thefamouspeople.com/profiles/epictetus-1350.php

Why Socrates Hated Democracy -. Retrieved 19
November 2020, from https://www.theschooloflife.
com/thebookoflife/why-socrates-hated-democracy/

Youtube. (2016). Retrieved 15 November 2020, from
https://www.youtube.com/watch?v=MgotDFs6cdE

Made in United States
Troutdale, OR
11/10/2024

24609561R20159